Gangs

Look for these and other books in the Lucent Overview Series:

Abortion
Acid Rain
Adoption
Advertising
Alcoholism
Animal Rights
Artificial Organs
The Beginning of Writing
The Brain
Cancer
Censorship
Child Abuse
Children's Rights
Cities
Cloning
The Collapse of the Soviet Union
Cults
Dealing with Death
Death Penalty
Democracy
Depression
Diabetes
Drug Abuse
Drugs and Sports
Drug Trafficking
Eating Disorders
Elections
Endangered Species
The End of Apartheid in South Africa
Energy Alternatives
Epidemics
Espionage
Ethnic Violence
Euthanasia
Extraterrestrial Life
Family Violence
Gangs
Garbage
Gay Rights
Genetic Engineering
The Greenhouse Effect
Gun Control
Hate Groups

Hazardous Waste
Health Care
The Holocaust
Homeless Children
Homelessness
Illegal Immigration
Illiteracy
Immigration
Juvenile Crime
Memory
Mental Illness
Militias
Money
Ocean Pollution
Oil Spills
The Olympic Games
Organ Transplants
Ozone
The Palestinian-Israeli Accord
Pesticides
Police Brutality
Population
Poverty
Prisons
Rainforests
The Rebuilding of Bosnia
Recycling
The Reunification of Germany
Schools
Smoking
Space Exploration
Special Effects in the Movies
Sports in America
Suicide
The UFO Challenge
The United Nations
The U.S. Congress
The U.S. Presidency
Vanishing Wetlands
Vietnam
Women's Rights
World Hunger
Zoos

Gangs

by Lisa Wolff

Lucent
Books

DISCARDED

LUCENT Overview Series

Library of Congress Cataloging-in-Publication Data

Wolff, Lisa, 1954–
      Gangs / by Lisa Wolff.
          p.   cm. — (Lucent overview series)
      Includes bibliographical references and index.
      Summary: Discusses gangs and their various aspects, including
the reasons why people join them, their relationship to crime, their
effects on society, and the prevention of gang-related crime.
      ISBN 1-56006-660-1 (lib. bdg. : alk. paper)
      1. Gangs—United States—Juvenile literature. 2. Gangs members—
United States—Social conditions Juvenile literature. 3. Gang
prevention—United States Juvenile literature. 4. Juvenile
delinquency—United States—Prevention Juvenile literature. [1. Gangs]
I. Title.   II. Series.
HV6439.U5W65   2000
364.1'06'609973—dc21   99-39714
                                                                                    CIP

Contents

Introduction

GANGS POSE A serious problem for American society. Despite an overall drop in the U.S. crime rate, gang-related crime remains high. A nationwide survey by the U.S. Department of Justice in 1996 showed that gang problems were getting worse in about 50 percent of communities. A 1997 Federal Bureau of Investigation (FBI) report states that gang membership in the nation had grown to about six hundred thousand by that year and that violent street gangs were operating in 94 percent of all medium-size and large cities. While fewer than half of American cities reported gang activity twenty years ago, it now appears to exist in every major city.

Early gangs

Street gangs are not a new problem; they have a long and troubling history in the United States. The earliest known American gangs formed in the 1780s, just after the end of the Revolutionary War. Like their contemporary counterparts, most gang members in the republic's early years were young men in their teens and twenties. While they, too, fought to defend their territory, these early gang members usually held jobs and few were involved in serious criminal activity.

Gangs became a much greater social problem in the nineteenth century, when the U.S. economy was in decline and the nation's growing populace was competing for a limited number of jobs. Among those most affected by the difficult social and economic conditions were European immigrants who settled with others from their own country in crowded urban areas. Unwelcome by the American majority, they often had trouble getting decent jobs and earning respect. Many were unable to find jobs at all and were left feeling angry and hopeless. In response, some immigrants came together to form street gangs; crime became a way of survival for them as many "earned" their living by robbing.

In New York City, young Irishmen formed the earliest criminal gangs. As other immigrant groups arrived in America's cities, they also formed gangs, and rival gangs often fought each other. By the late 1860s New York City had Irish, Italian, Jewish, and African American gangs, and

In the United States, gangs have been traced back to the late 1700s. This photo of New York City's "Short Tail Gang" was taken in 1890.

Chinese gangs had surfaced in California. Each of these gangs formed its own identity, often with special colors and styles of dress. Some assembled on street corners and committed minor crimes in their own territory or were simply a public nuisance; others specialized in burglarizing and vandalizing homes. Weapons and fighting became an important part of gang life.

As the gap between rich and poor in American cities widened in the early twentieth century, gang activity increased, and the use of guns became more widespread. Gang warfare—gunfights between rival gangs—became a serious problem in the 1920s. Gang activity spread from the cities of the East Coast to midwestern cities like Chicago and western cities like Los Angeles. The 1950s saw the rise of girl gangs and the increasing role of drugs in gang culture. During the 1990s, the number of gangs increased in smaller cities and in suburbs.

Gangs today

Historically, gang members have tended to be young and poor, to live in crowded urban areas, and to feel they have little opportunity to advance in American society. Today, as in years past, they turn to others like themselves—young people of the same race, nationality, and social class—for support and guidance. Gangs give them a sense of belonging in the world and a feeling of power. Members often feel alienated from their families, the school system, and society in general. They reject society's rules and follow their own. They typically use violence as a means of both protecting their territory and gaining money and power.

Today more than ever, weapons and drugs are a central feature of gang culture in the United States. The easy availability of guns, and an increasing willingness to use them, have made gangs even more dangerous to the general population than in the past as innocent people—often children—fall victim to gang violence in drive-by shootings. Drugs, and the enormous amounts of money generated by their sale, have also increased gang violence. While in the past much of this violence was between rival gangs, it is

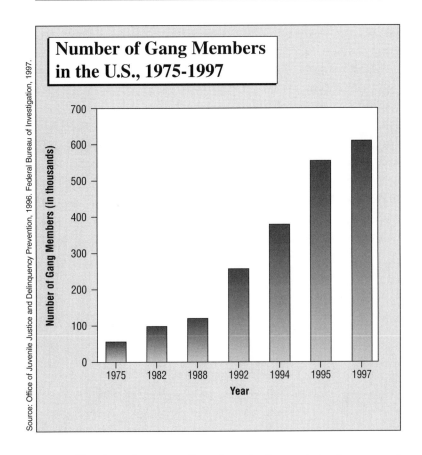

Source: Office of Juvenile Justice and Delinquency Prevention, 1996. Federal Bureau of Investigation, 1997.

Number of Gang Members in the U.S., 1975-1997

Number of Gang Members (in thousands)

Year

now affecting the rest of society to the point where most Americans agree that gang crime is a serious problem in this country.

While there is agreement on the problem, there are different opinions on the best way to solve it. Some people favor harsh penalties for gang-related crime, such as long prison sentences and the sentencing of violent juvenile offenders as adults. However, others do not see punishment as the solution. They view gangs as a natural outgrowth of certain social conditions that need correction: poverty, overcrowded conditions in inner-city neighborhoods, the collapse of the family, problems with the educational system, and racial and ethnic prejudice. For young people whose lives seem hopeless, they note, gangs serve as substitute families, offering a sense of security and social acceptance as well as economic opportunity not found in the greater society. Until these conditions change, critics say, gang culture will continue to flourish despite all of the justice system's efforts to eradicate it.

Whatever the proposed approach, most people agree that wiping out gang-related crime will not be easy. As long as young people feel powerless and angry, many are likely to continue to join gangs. And as long as there is money to be made through criminal activity like selling drugs, gang members will continue to commit crimes that threaten American society. Understanding what leads people to join gangs is the first step toward finding ways to deal with one of the nation's most complex social problems.

1

The Appeal of Gangs

THROUGHOUT HISTORY MOST gang members have been young males from poor families. Most have grown up in urban areas, and many are part of a racial or ethnic minority group that is not fully integrated in American society. Recent immigrants are popular targets for gangs that are recruiting new members.

However, not all gang members are poor, urban, or members of minority groups. Some are white suburban youths from middle-class families. A rise in racist "skinhead" gangs is a signal that the problems leading to gang membership are widespread in the United States. There has also been a rise in female gangs, though one study estimates that 90 percent of gang members are male.

On the surface, gangs provide young people with a sense of purpose. They promise a support system to kids with absentee parents, jobs to the poorly educated, and both easy money and material rewards. One of the main traits gang members share is a feeling of hopelessness—that there is no place for them in American society outside of the gang. For young people with neither skills nor adult guidance, gangs offer a clearly defined route toward gaining respect and earning money and power.

Though gangs vary widely in size and structure, all live by a set of well-defined rules. The largest gangs, located in major cities, have as many as two thousand members; these members divide into smaller groups, called clubs or cliques. Gangs in smaller cities or towns tend to be much smaller, though they may have ties to a large urban group.

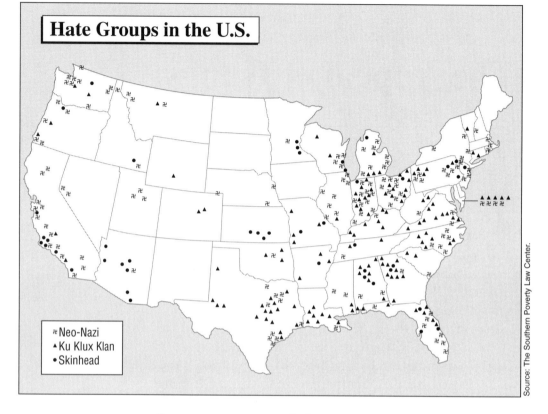

Hate Groups in the U.S.

ℵ Neo-Nazi
▲ Ku Klux Klan
● Skinhead

Source: The Southern Poverty Law Center.

Some gangs operate informally, with alternating leaders; others are highly structured, with strong leaders and officers who have clearly defined duties.

Despite their differences, the basic nature of all gangs is the same. Members must obey a strict code of behavior and follow the gangs' rules; in turn, the gangs provide members with protection and a sense of security. Gangs demand loyalty of their members, and the penalties for breaking the rules are often severe. However, they promise great rewards to loyal members who live by their laws. Successful gang members gain money, power, prestige, and an opportunity to move up in the ranks.

This sense of structure and security makes joining gangs particularly appealing to young people who feel powerless at home, in school, and in society in general. Gangs convince such teens that their lives have value. They provide work and money, though often through stealing or selling drugs. They offer protection from others in the neighborhood who may threaten them. They command respect through fear and intimidation. And for teens from families with serious problems, they offer a substitute family.

There are many factors that lure troubled children and teens into joining gangs. One factor is the glamorous and exciting image of gangs in popular culture. Kids whose futures seem grim are often drawn to these images, which seem to promise an escape from their depressing situations.

Gangs in the media

Gangs have been the subject of movies for decades. In 1961, *West Side Story* retold one of the most romantic tales of all time—Shakespeare's *Romeo and Juliet*—as a struggle between two warring New York City gangs. Though there is no direct evidence that *West Side Story* drew any of its audience into gang life, many teens embraced the hairstyles,

Many people feel that gang life has been glamorized by movies such as West Side Story.

jeans, and black leather jackets the actors playing the gang members wore.

Some people blame the media for making gangs seem cool to kids. Critics complain that movies portray gang members as adventurous outlaws instead of violent criminals. *Colors,* a 1988 movie about Los Angeles gangs, has been criticized for glamorizing gang life and encouraging children to join gangs. The film employed as extras real members of two Los Angeles gangs, the Bloods and the Crips, and theaters gave patrons bandannas in the gang colors as part of their promotion. As an officer in the Albuquerque, New Mexico, police department observed, "While the movie was a factual portrayal of gang life, kids thought it made gang life glamorous. And the movie theaters' promoting the film by handing out red and blue bandannas made it worse."[1]

The few studies that have been conducted on the effects of media violence on young people have not proven a clear connection between what children see and hear and how they act. However, some children and teens admit to being directly influenced by the portrayal of gangs on television and in the movies. An eighteen-year-old member of a New York gang recalls, "I was just sitting watching television and the news was on when they did this segment on one of the gangs. These brothers were bad. . . . So I decided to check it out and I joined. . . . I might have joined another club, but I wouldn't have joined this one if it hadn't been for what they said in that TV program. They had it down, man!"[2]

Although there is no hard evidence of a connection, many members of the law enforcement community have observed what they believe is a link between the popular images kids see of gangs and their desire to belong to those gangs. Sergeant Peter Ritter, a supervisor of the Gang Investigation Unit of the Boise Police Department in Idaho, asserts that "most of the information area kids are getting about gangs is off CDs and the movies. That is what has lent some social acceptance to belonging to a street gang."[3]

Music with violent lyrics is another form of entertainment often cited as an influence on children and teens.

Many people feel that the lyrics of such "gangsta rap" groups as NWA (pictured) encourage young people to join gangs.

Some people believe the music encourages young people to join gangs or participate in gang-related crime. Music has been blamed for inciting white gangs to commit crimes against minority groups, and rap music has been singled out as portraying violent activity as the norm for young residents of inner cities.

Rap and heavy metal music about rebelling against society can make gang attitudes and criminal activity seem normal to some children and teens. Movies and television shows that depict gang members as handsome, daring, loyal, and respected can make gang life look exciting while ignoring the way it ruins lives. Many critics fear that these images can be a powerful lure for impressionable young people.

But the outward appeal of gangs—their colorful dress, secret codes, and glamorized media image—is seldom the only factor that attracts kids. Another major reason why many young people join gangs is found at home.

Peer pressure to join gangs

Gangs are a powerful force in many communities. In urban neighborhoods where gang activity is common, the pressure to join a gang can be overwhelming. Many children and teens have brothers and friends who are gang members. Even those who do not have friends or relatives in gangs may feel pressured by others in the neighborhood, particularly older boys who act as father figures to children from broken homes. Young people may feel not only pressured to join a gang but also threatened if they refuse to join.

Those who fail to join may be treated as outcasts or even as traitors. In minority neighborhoods, they may be taunted for identifying with the white middle-class society that is viewed by many gang members as the enemy. By following the rules of the greater society—going to school, earning good grades, avoiding illegal activity, and preparing for white-collar jobs—they are condemned for "selling out."

In some inner-city neighborhoods, the block on which a boy lives may be controlled by a gang, and the accident of growing up on this "turf" may determine his future. His friends and neighbors may convince him that the local gang represents his heritage and roots in the community: It defines his identity in society. Gang members stress that the greater society does not want these poor minority youths, that it is denying them a share of its prosperity. Therefore, their only place is in this subculture, the neighborhood gang that will protect them and reward them for their loyalty.

For some children, gang membership is not only a common neighborhood custom but also a family tradition. In certain cultures, several generations of family members may be gang members.

Gangs as a family tradition

While lack of a strong family structure leads many young people to join gangs, children who grow up in families with gang members often join gangs to be closer to their family members. A boy whose father, grandfather, and uncles all belong to a gang is almost doomed to continue in their footsteps. Loyalty to the family's gang is expected and encouraged, and breaking away will alienate him from those he loves.

Generations of membership is particularly common among Hispanic gangs. In the barrios of Southern California, boys are often considered born into gangs. A writer on youth and family issues observes, "Fathers, uncles, and grandfathers have been 'soldiers' for the barrio gang. There is even a name for the old-timers: veteranos, the thirty-, forty-, and fifty-year-old members of the gang. The younger ones are taught by the older members before taking their place in this senseless battlefield. They, in time, will teach still younger ones."[4]

In these gangs, the most experienced members—usually the oldest ones—are looked up to as leaders. A boy whose father or grandfather is a powerful figure in the gang is likely to carry on the family tradition. A seventeen-year-old member of a Los Angeles gang describes his connection to a local Hispanic gang: "A lot of people in the community have been in it. I had lots of family in it so I guess I'll have to carry on the tradition. A lot of people from outside this community wouldn't understand, but we have helped the community whenever they've asked us. . . . I felt it's kind of my duty to join because everyone expects it."[5]

Girls born into gang families are sometimes drawn in as well. A twenty-year-old former member of the Vice Lords, who drifted away from the gang when she had a child, describes her uncles: "They were proud to be Vice Lords. They'd talk to us sometimes, especially when we got to the age where we wanted to be in the gang too. They'd tell us stories about the gang when they were young. They'd give us advice, too, about what to do."[6]

Even in families where the older generation is not part of a gang, boys may be persuaded to join by an older brother or cousin or by older neighborhood boys. In these situations, a strong father figure is often absent, and the older boy assumes the father role.

Gangs as a substitute family

Many gang members come from single-parent families, and the loyalty they can expect in a gang, as well as the clearly defined set of rules, often represent more consistent care than they receive in their own homes. The gang takes over the role of the parents, providing rules, guidance, and discipline. For children who receive inconsistent treatment at home due to parental drug or alcohol abuse, the strict set of rules a gang provides is often a relief in an otherwise confusing life. Abused and neglected children are at especially high risk of getting involved in criminal activity. The U.S. Department of Justice reports that they are forty times more likely than other children to be arrested as juveniles or adults.

In fact, many people who study youth gangs see the increase in single-parent families as a major factor in gang membership. Approximately one-quarter of American families are now headed by one parent, usually the mother, and the percentage rises to one-third among Hispanic families and one-half among black families. The Centers for Disease Control report that 85 percent of children with behavioral problems come from fatherless homes. These children, they note, are nine times more likely to drop out of high school, ten times more likely to use drugs, and

twenty times more likely to end up in prison. Many of them gravitate toward gangs, often looking to older gang members as father figures.

Brotherhood and the sense of community

Laron Douglas, a member of the Chicago gang Black Gangster Disciples, joined for this reason. He notes, "Being in this glorious organization has taught me a lot. I grew up without a father and I turned to my Disciple brothaz [brothers] for love. They know exactly how to treat a brotha and were always there for me, through thick and thin."[7]

In addition to the guidance of father figures, many gang members are attracted by the gang's sense of community. The gang is a place where they feel accepted and are encouraged to make a contribution to the community—both within the gang itself and in the neighborhood.

Gang leaders often convince their members that the gang plays an important role in the neighborhood, keeping the streets safe from outsiders. This gives young members a sense of purpose and helps create a spirit of loyalty within the group as they work together toward a common goal.

While gang members see themselves as an important part of the community, they also create their own community inside the neighborhood. Within the greater society, from which many young people feel alienated, they provide a smaller, secret society that makes its members feel part of a special group. Gang rituals—particular ways of dressing, communicating, and behaving—are an important part of their communal appeal.

Rules and rituals

The outward trappings of gang life—the uniforms with their special colors, the tattoos, graffiti, and signals—attract many young people. They give them a sense of belonging to a secret society, making them feel special. Gang symbols and rites often look cool to teens who are seeking an identity. Such rites distinguish gang members in a society that does not seem to offer a place for them, and they link them to others like themselves—usually kids who are poor, of the same race or ethnic group, and are growing up in a crowded, dangerous urban environment.

Most gangs use their own combination of symbols and behaviors for identification and a sense of belonging. They develop a certain way of dress, often with special gang colors, that lets them identify fellow members and distinguishes them from other gangs. They create a sort of code language that they use in their graffiti—stylized words, numbers, and symbols that they write or spray paint on walls and other surfaces. Graffiti, or "tags," mark gang territory and warn other gangs to stay away. When members of rival gangs paint over each other's graffiti, gang wars often follow. Other gang rituals include the use of special hand signals, a sort of sign language.

Gang violence is also used as a ritual to initiate new members. By committing a violent act on behalf of the gang, a new member is pledging his loyalty. Gang violence acts as a bonding experience, bringing members closer to each other because of the shared risk and the need to protect fellow members. Researchers writing about the gang violence that was committed against two college students as part of an ini-

Crips gang members flash the signals unique to their gang.

tiation rite observe that "the recruits who actually conducted the violence, the leaders who ordered and observed the violence, and those who were later told the recruits 'did good,' were all sharing in the violence—they all felt somewhat united as a result of the violent actions of just two recruits."[8]

Often, new members are initiated by being forced to fight members of their own gang. This process, called "jumping in," allows all important members to witness the recruit's fighting abilities and bravery.

Each type of gang develops its own set of rituals. Its style of dress, symbols, and behavior often have ties to its members' community and culture. For example, Hispanic gangs generally assume street names that are related to their neighborhoods, of which they consider themselves protectors. White skinhead gangs advertise their racism by patterning their dress after the Nazis and wearing swastika tattoos.

The appeal of the organization

One of the main appeals of gangs is their social structure. While many young people are rebelling against society, they are also seeking a structure—a set of rules by which to live—that can replace the social rules they reject. It is important for them to find a place where they seem to belong and are accepted. For many, gangs provide that place.

Street gangs offer a ladder that young members can climb toward success within the group by pledging their loyalty and following the rules. An eighteen-year-old former member of the Crips, who was blinded in a gunfight, notes, "There's a definite organization to a gang. You start as a soldier, no rank. As you grow, you accomplish things in the gang, so you get promoted."[9]

When their needs are not met, children are likely to seek the support of a group outside of the home: other neighborhood kids growing up in similar circumstances. As a fifteen-year-old observed after his first year of membership in an Irish gang, "Before I joined the gang, I could see that you could count on your boys to help in times of need and that meant a lot to me. And when I needed money, sure enough they gave it to me. . . . The gang was just like they said they would be, and they'll continue to be there when I need them."[10]

Perhaps even more appealing to many young people than the rituals and sense of belonging that are a part of gang life are the promised rewards of loyal membership. These include both the material rewards of financial gain and the respect that many gang members seem to command in the neighborhood. Another reward is the protection of fellow gang members against those of rival gangs.

The rewards of gang membership

For children and teens growing up in troubled neighborhoods, the temptation to join a gang is strong. They probably have friends and classmates who already belong and who have material possessions—money, jewelry, expensive sneakers—that they covet. For children who have little and whose prospects in life seem dim, gangs offer a glamorous, potentially rewarding choice. As a former member of a Boston gang observes, "You know, it's like the badder you are, the more status you have. . . . If you're out here sellin' drugs, the kids see it, and they see the fancy cars, they see, you know, that you're out there every day, don't have to work real hard, you got all the gold, the leather coats, your life looks great."[11]

Beyond these possessions, the gang members appear to command respect in the neighborhood. They also offer protection against others in the neighborhood who prey on vulnerable kids. Stanley "Tookie" Williams, who co-founded the notorious Crips gang in 1971, notes that "there were so many gangs prevalent during that era and in our neighborhoods, that we had to band together against them to protect each other and to protect our family members, our loved ones."[12]

The promise of respect

To kids whose futures seem to hold little prospect, even the likely consequences of gang life may not look negative. In a culture where men frequently go to prison, spending time behind bars seems to some a badge of honor. To them,

it represents being tough, "taking it like a man." Williams describes one of his childhood role models, Rock, who spoke with pride of the years he spent in prison: "He said prisons were places where a man could prove his toughness to other men who were equally tough."[13]

A former gang member in Richmond, California, who now counsels young people in the neighborhood, had similar negative role models. He recalls, "When I was growing up, we all looked up to people in jail and stuff like that. I wish I had someone to say 'hey you know what, if you go to school you can be something. If you keep hanging out in the streets, you're gonna keep getting in trouble with the police' . . . and telling me the consequences."[14]

Gang members often join a gang for protection and a feeling of camaraderie.

Joining gangs for protection

In a crime-ridden neighborhood, the need for protection is a major motive for joining a gang. Street gangs promise to take care of their members—to provide them with arms and to back them up in a fight against members of a rival gang. Children who have been threatened or robbed on their way home from school see great appeal in an older gang member's offer of protection.

John Garbarino, director of the Family Life Development Center at Cornell University, describes the attitude of many troubled youths today: "Kids have a declining confidence in the future. They've given up on the ability of adults to protect them. A kid in Michigan once said to me, 'If I join a gang, I'm 50 percent safe. If I don't join a gang, I'm zero percent safe.'"[15]

Many children growing up in America's inner cities believe that joining a gang is the only way to be safe on their local streets. A sixteen-year-old member of a Los Angeles gang describes the scenario: "Man, I joined the Fultons because there are a lot of people who are trying to get you and if you don't get protection you are in trouble sometimes. My homeboys gave me protection, so they were the thing to do."[16]

Teens like this fail to realize that joining a gang actually exposes them to greater danger. As part of a gang, they automatically make many dangerous enemies in the form of rival gang members. These enemies are typically armed and ready for a fight with their rivals. Wearing gang colors or using the gang's signs or graffiti makes a member a target for the opposition. They are signals that the gang member is ready to fight if provoked.

2

Gangs, Drugs, and Violence

GANGS AND CRIME go hand in hand. In fact, the FBI considers criminal activity to be part of the definition of a gang:

> Participation in criminal activity is what separates community groups or social clubs from gangs. For instance, a motorcycle club that has initiation rituals, an organizational structure (for example, club president, vice president, etc.), and wears similar clothing ("colors") is NOT viewed as a gang by the FBI unless the club and its members become involved in criminal activity.[17]

The criminal activity of gangs grows out of their very nature. Gang members tend to see themselves as being outside of the law; instead, they follow "laws" of their own. Gangs have been associated with crime since the nineteenth century. Gangs today, however, are far more violent than in the past. The widespread use of automatic and semiautomatic guns has changed the nature of gang violence. With gangs using deadlier weapons, and with their shootings claiming more innocent victims, many Americans consider gang violence to be a national crisis.

A major factor in gang violence is drugs. The booming drug market of the 1980s and 1990s dramatically increased the incidence of gang-related crime and violence. The enormous profits at stake in the drug trade compel gang members to risk their lives—along with the lives of others—in the struggle over drug turf. That struggle has become increasingly deadly, and the FBI reports that gang violence is now responsible for 10 to 30 percent of all homicides in major urban areas.

Many people see gang violence as a reflection of American society. Throughout the nation's history, people have used weapons to settle disputes and exert power over others.

A heritage of violence

Americans have a heritage of violence dating all the way back to the seventeenth century, when the first settlers arrived and believed it was their right to take over the land. This culture of violence continued over the centuries as settlers headed west, expanding their territory. They claimed territory by a show of force, using guns to drive others out. In this atmosphere, many refused to live by the laws of the country or state and became known as outlaws. Outlaws in the Wild West are part of the romantic American legend. They are often glamorized on television and in movies, and little boys grow up pretending to be Jesse James or Billy the Kid—bank robbers and killers who played by their own rules.

Many kids today, particularly gang members, have embraced these popular images and view themselves as outlaws. They may see this culture of violence reflected in their own homes in the form of physically abusive parents as well as on their neighborhood streets. In urban ghettos, gang members are raised in the shadow of robberies, drug shootouts, and police raids, and they often consider this situation a valid reason to steal, destroy property, fight, and even kill. They see anyone who crosses them as the enemy, and they deal with these enemies through violence and the threat of violence.

In addition, children today are surrounded by violence in the media. Shootouts in movies and on television are commonplace, with action-adventure programming promoted to boys and teens. Rock, and especially rap, music blasts messages about violent revenge. This barrage of images makes violence seem like a normal part of life.

While violence has always been a part of American culture, the level soared in the 1980s and 1990s with the spread of the drug trade. Many law enforcement officials attribute much of the increase in violent urban crime in the late 1980s to drugs—specifically, to crack cocaine.

Crack cocaine

Crack, a smokable, less concentrated, and less expensive form of cocaine, quickly became the drug of choice in poor urban neighborhoods in the 1980s. As Billy Stewart, a Boston probation officer, notes, "Crack was probably the catalyst for the explosion of violence in the city of Boston. Crack and the profits that people derive from it. With those profits you got to have guns to protect your profits. Crack almost brought this city to its knees. We were dying around here because of it."[18]

Two Los Angeles police officers confiscate crack cocaine from a member of the "Wet Town" gang.

Gang members had no trouble distributing the drug to their neighbors, creating a great concentration of addiction and crime in the inner cities. Violent crime rose both among the crack addicts themselves and the drug dealers, who fought over valuable sales territories.

Given the ready supply, many gang members use crack and other drugs themselves. However, some gangs discourage drug use among their members, and some even prohibit the use of certain drugs, such as heroin, that lead users to act unpredictably and put the gang at risk. A twenty-year-old member of a New York gang observes that "no one wants to have anybody who is on heroin in the gang because you need to be able to trust one of your gang brothers and everyone knows that a heroin addict owes his soul to the pusher. The only thing you can count on from a junky is that he will find a way to score, and you can't run an efficient organization with people like that."[19]

Drugs and money

Once street gangs got involved with the drug trade, it quickly became their main source of income and the motive for most of their killing. Today, drug trafficking is the most frequently reported crime among most types of gangs.

Black Gangster Disciples member Laron Douglas, like many of his fellow gang members, sees drug dealing as the easiest solution to inner-city poverty. He notes, "The dope game is a way to get quick money, and the brothaz see this, you know, living in the ghetto. They don't have too much, and selling drugs gives them the chance to have the finer things in life. . . . We do appreciate legit [legitimate] professions, but living in the ghetto is hard so we got to start somewhere and move up."[20]

Drug dealing among gangs has become a sophisticated business, with a structure much like that of many legitimate American companies. A 1998 study published by the National Bureau of Economic Research reveals that a typical gang has a leader and a few officers at the top, followed by twenty-five to seventy-five "foot soldiers" selling drugs on the street and sixty to two hundred members who pay dues in exchange for gang protection and a reliable supply of drugs. According to this study, gang leaders made $50,000 to $130,000 per year during the height of the crack cocaine epidemic in the late 1980s and early 1990s, and gangs' profits doubled as they expanded their turf. It also showed the high price paid for dealing drugs: Gang members had a one-in-four chance of dying over the four-year period studied.

Today, selling drugs is the largest moneymaking activity among gangs, and most gangs compete for part of the drug

Beatrice Codianni Robles, the "Director of Programs and Charter Goals" for the Latin Kings gang, was sentenced to seventeen years in prison for ordering a hit on a rival drug dealer.

market. In cities such as New York, the older and larger gangs control more of the market than the traditional supplier of illegal drugs, organized crime. These gangs are able to buy drugs from suppliers and distribute them to the people who sell them on the street. This way, gangs avoid selling directly to the drug users—a practice that has the highest risk of arrest. Instead, gang members commonly hire children at low pay to act as street sellers, and the gangs keep most of the profits.

In addition to buying drugs from the people who smuggle them in from other parts of the world, some New York City and Los Angeles gangs are producing their own drugs. They set up drug mills where they manufacture such drugs as LSD and crack cocaine to sell on the street, generating large profits. Other gangs pay pharmacy employees to steal pills—which are legal but available only by prescription—for them to sell on the street.

One of the effects of the increase in drug use has been the spread of gangs into new areas. The great profit to be made in the drug trade has led them to constantly seek new clients. Once various gangs have met the demands of an entire city, they branch out into new markets.

The spread of drugs throughout America

Across the country, the spread of the drug trade has been linked to the spread of gangs. Criminal gang activity, once largely confined to inner cities, is now seen even in quiet rural communities. This invasion of once-safe neighborhoods has sounded an alarm among citizens and their elected government representatives.

In a 1997 address to Congress, Vermont senator Patrick Leahy expressed the concern of his state in a proposal for the Youth Violence, Crime, and Drug Abuse Bill. Noting that 64 percent more juveniles were arrested for violent crimes in 1995 than in 1987, he stated,

> Concern about the spread of gangs—and the violence, the drug dealing and other criminal activity gangs leave in their wake—has spread from our large cities to rural American towns. Indeed, one of the major factors responsible for the increases in

States Reporting the Most Gang Members

1. California
2. Illinois
3. Texas
4. Ohio
5. Indiana
6. New Mexico
7. Arizona
8. Florida
9. Nevada
10. Minnesota

Note: New York City's police department did not participate in the survey.

Source: U. S. Department of Justice, 1996.

juvenile crime over the past decade is the growth of criminal street gangs across this country. Although places such as Los Angeles and New York first spring to mind when the word "gang" is mentioned, gangs are spreading across the nation indiscriminately.[21]

A 1995 study by the National Gang Crime Research Center in Chicago observed the spread of the Black Gangster Disciples, a major Chicago gang, into thirty-five other states. The center's director, George Knox, noted that the main factor in this migration was drugs. According to Knox, gang members first visit a new city with an untapped drug market and then move in: "They see there's nothing happening, see dollar signs, set up a prototype, and they're up and running. It's sort of like a McDonald's operation, a franchise."[22]

Police in Springfield, Missouri, discovered a large Gangster Disciple "franchise" in their community in 1993.

Arrested gang members explained that they could sell a rock of cocaine for fifty dollars in Springfield that would normally sell for only ten to twenty-five dollars in Chicago. Until the competition moves in, gangs can make an enormous profit in a new drug market.

Two major Los Angeles gangs, the Crips and the Bloods, are well known for their drug dealing and violence. Offshoots of these gangs have been showing up in small cities in the Midwest, as well as other parts of the country, to exploit the spreading demand for drugs. Crips and Bloods now control drug operation bases in Seattle, Portland, Omaha, Kansas City, and Minneapolis.

As gang members became major drug traffickers, the level of violence among street gangs soared. The enormous amounts of money involved in selling illegal drugs has led to intense competition among gangs to control their part of the market and expand into new ones.

The increased involvement of street gangs in the illegal drug trade coincided with the spread of guns among gang members. With so much valuable merchandise to protect, gang leaders made sure that their members were well armed. Gangs carefully guard their drug-selling territories. Guns are the most effective way of keeping rival gang members out as well as getting revenge against those who cross the lines.

Guns and violence

Because selling drugs is an illegal activity, drug dealers do not have legal recourse when rival gang members interfere with their business practices. They therefore rely on violence to protect their territory and profits. As a 1992 Bureau of Justice Statistics report notes,

> In the drug world, buyers and sellers rely only on their own resources to enforce contracts. Violence is often the only effective preventive measure against unfair trade practices. A dealer, especially when selling to a new buyer, risks having his drugs stolen and even being killed. . . . A reputation for violence is the dealer's best guarantee that his business transaction will be accomplished as agreed upon. Once the reputation for violence is established, it is not as necessary to continue violent acts to protect transactions.[23]

The spread of guns into what were previously considered to be safe areas has alarmed many people and attracted a great deal of media attention. However, the majority of violent gang crime remains concentrated in large cities. In 1994 just four cities—Chicago, Los Angeles, New York, and Detroit—accounted for nearly one-third of all juvenile homicide arrests in the United States.

Still, the random nature of gang shootings, which often claim the lives of innocent bystanders, raises special concerns throughout the country. One of the main concerns is about how easily gang members are able to obtain guns.

Easy access to guns

Like violence, gun ownership and use has a long history in the United States. Even many law-abiding citizens own guns, both for sport and for protection, and the majority believe that they should have this right. The right to bear arms was written into the U.S. Constitution in the eighteenth century, and Americans are reluctant to give it up, even as they witness senseless killings during a drive-by shooting. The United States has some of the most permissive gun laws in the world, and many Americans are determined to keep them that way. Gun sales are a big business, and guns are extremely easy to buy.

There are now an estimated 250 million guns in the United States, with 4.5 million new guns sold each year. Many of these guns are sold illegally and fall into the hands of gang members. Gang members are killing each other in great numbers as well as ending the lives of many people who happen to get caught in the crossfire. They are also killing, and getting killed, at a younger age. Every day about thirteen children under age nineteen are killed by gunfire.

Even in suburban and rural areas, guns have been getting into the hands of young gang members. In 1999, documentary filmmaker Enrique Cerna investigated the story of a thirteen-year-old boy in prison for shooting a rival gang member in a small Washington State farming community. Cerna observes, "In a way, we've all become a little desensitized. It's not so

Members of the Los Angeles Crips gang display their arsenal of weapons.

much a big deal to pick up the paper and read about a drive-by where a young kid was involved. The access to guns that kids have, their willingness to use them . . . it's really frightening."[24]

Gangs have little trouble assembling an arsenal of weapons. While some gang members steal guns, most buy them from wholesale gun dealers and resell them for a profit. Some gangs—particularly Irish gangs—make large amounts of money from the resale of illegal guns. Their high demand for these weapons prompts gun manufacturers to increase their supply.

Many people blame the manufacturers and sellers of guns for allowing the weapons to get into the hands of minors and criminals. Some are also trying to hold parents responsible for letting guns fall into their children's hands.

Responsibility for gun violence

In 1998 the rise in gang-related killings led parents in Chicago to file a lawsuit against gun makers, accusing them of targeting gang members in the sale of guns. The parents, whose children had been killed by juveniles carrying handguns, claimed that the weapons were marketed to meet the demands of criminal gang members. Advertising for the guns stressed their high-volume firepower and fingerprint resistance, factors that appeal to criminals. Many critics of American gun laws note that automatic and semiautomatic weapons are geared toward committing crimes, not hunting or self-defense. These weapons spray bullets and are often used to clear a street corner of rival gang members rather than hit a specific target.

Individuals, groups, counties, and even cities in several states filed similar lawsuits against gun manufacturers during 1998, drawing strong opposition from the National Rifle Association. As of May 1999, ten American cities and counties had filed such suits, seeking reimbursement for the costs of gun violence. In Texas, however, legislators passed a bill to prevent cities and counties from suing gun makers.

As shootings by children and teens rise, some critics are shifting the blame to parents. They are trying to hold the parents of juveniles who kill or injure with guns financially responsible for the crimes and, in some cases, are even seeking jail sentences.

Kids and guns: A deadly combination

Guns are also making their way into schools. As a result, students who attend schools with gang populations report being victims of violent crimes more often than students who attend gang-free schools. The presence of armed gangs at schools has prompted other children to arm themselves for self-protection. Many schools in troubled urban neighborhoods require students to pass through metal detectors to prevent guns and knives from being brought to class.

Between 1984 and 1994, the number of juvenile homicides in the United States tripled; likewise, the number of children who committed homicide using guns quadrupled, accounting for nearly 80 percent of all youth homicides in

1994. Today, more teenage boys are killed by guns than by all natural causes combined. Homicide is the leading cause of death among black males under the age of twenty-five. Much of this killing is in gang-related violence, usually over drugs or territory.

In addition to having more—and more powerful—weapons, gang members are using them more freely. Because gang members are younger than ever—some as young as eight years old—their attitude toward guns is often unrealistic. As James Fox, the author of a Northeastern University study on violent crime, observes, "A 45-year-old with a gun in his hand, although he may be a better shot, is not as likely to use that gun as a 14-year-old. Fourteen-year-olds tend to be trigger-happy. . . . They'll pull that trigger if someone swears at them. They'll pull that trigger without thinking about the consequences."[25]

Gang violence and the future

Since the 1980s and 1990s, gangs have become increasingly violent due to the easy availability of powerful weapons and the enormous profits of the drug trade.

As gangs expand their drug territory to new areas, this violence affects a much larger part of society than ever before. Few large towns or cities have escaped the threat of gang violence, and even some rural areas are experiencing drug dealing and gang warfare on a smaller scale.

Although gang violence is spreading to new areas, its greatest concentration remains among the urban poor. Many observers do not expect this to change unless there is a major effort to help these communities. As Elijah Anderson, a professor of social science at the University of Pennsylvania, comments, "The inclination of violence springs from the circumstances of life among the ghetto poor—the lack of jobs that pay a living wage, the stigma of race, the fallout from rampant drug use and drug trafficking, and the resulting alienation and lack of hope for the future."[26]

3

Life in a Gang-Infested Neighborhood

IN THE LATE 1980s, as guns flooded the streets of many urban neighborhoods, there was a sharp rise in gang-related killings. In Boston, where gang violence reached crisis levels, most shootings occurred in three neighborhoods where gangs overlapped and fought over drug territory. Disputes that were once settled with fists were settled with bullets. These shootings also claimed the lives of anyone who got in the way. A boy interviewed for a television documentary on youth gangs describes the mood of violence in Boston's inner-city neighborhoods: "Anybody could shoot you, for the wrong look you could get shot. You could get shot for wearing Nike, you could get shot for anything."[27]

To most outsiders, a gang appears to be a primarily destructive force. Though it provides a substitute family for many kids with troubled home lives, its so-called family values are usually at odds with those of society. However, many gang members believe that they play positive roles in their communities. In dangerous inner-city neighborhoods, they take on the role of a self-styled police force. In many gang members' minds, they are performing a valuable public service, keeping their local streets safe from intruders—often members of rival gangs. As an eighteen-year-old gang member in New York notes, "I know, we all know, that people outside our neighborhood wouldn't think much of us. You know, we would just be nobodies to them, but here we are given respect by the people in the community, and that is because we do things for them. So if we want to keep some respect, we need [to] continue to help the people here."[28]

A sixteen-year-old member of the Gangster Disciples (GD) in Chicago expressed a similar view: "It's not all gangbanging and stuff like that. To me, GD could stand for Growth and Development. . . . It's, like, we're here to help out the neighborhood. We're more into protecting than anything else. It's a pride thing, pride and loyalty to the neighborhood where you live."[29]

It is not difficult to understand how some inner-city youths might feel this way about gang membership. Children who grow up in gang-ridden neighborhoods seem to be born with two strikes against them. Most live in poverty, with parents who are struggling to make a living, and attend troubled schools where getting a good education is a challenge. The streets they walk and the parks they play in are dangerous and threatening, often littered with needles and crack vials. They have few positive role models, and to many of these kids, the future looks bleak. Gang recruiters may convince them that joining a gang is a positive move and blind them to the ways in which gangs victimize families and neighborhoods.

The victims of gang violence

While much gang-related crime is targeted at rival gang members, its costs have a major impact on American society. The direct victims of gang violence suffer the most, but many others also experience the effects of crime and violence by gang members. The families of gang members are often torn apart as their children or brothers are sent to jail or killed by rivals. Neighborhoods where gang activity is a way of life live in fear. Schools are disrupted by gang violence. Communities targeted by gangs soon become infested with drugs.

The most immediate effects of crimes by gang members are felt by their victims. These include people who are hit by stray bullets during drive-by shootings as well as those who are injured or killed during a robbery or other crime. Some of the young victims of gangs are children and teens who are pressured into joining a local gang but refuse. They may be robbed or beaten, and gang members may threaten their lives. Anyone wearing the clothing of an enemy gang—even if he is not actually a gang member—is also a target of gang violence. Certain styles of clothing or brands of sneakers symbolize an enemy to gang members, who attack before they ask questions.

But perhaps the most far-reaching effect is the overall climate of fear that gang violence creates in many neighborhoods. Gangs and the dangers they pose strike fear in communities large and small throughout the nation.

The climate of fear

Today even small cities, suburbs, and towns have branches of the gangs that originated in metropolitan cities like New York and Los Angeles. The signs of local gang activity, such as the selling of drugs and the prevalence of

graffiti, seem to forecast the deterioration of neighborhoods.

However, the greatest fear remains in inner-city neighborhoods where gangs already hold power. Parents are
frightened by the gangs' influence on their children, who
are often lured or pressured into joining. They also fear
that these children will get caught in the crossfire of gang
wars or that they will be tempted to buy drugs from gang
dealers or to help them carry or sell drugs. In addition,
gangs in the inner cities have a strong impact on the lives
of older residents. In gang-infested neighborhoods, the elderly often become prisoners of their own homes, afraid to
go out on streets that are controlled by violent gangs.

The presence of gangs in these neighborhoods creates a
climate of general unease. It affects all residents: children
who have to pass groups of gang members on street corners on their way to school, workers who fear being crime
victims when they travel home after dark, and the owners
of businesses where gangs choose to congregate. Gabe
Gonzalez, executive director of the Northwest Neighborhood Federation in Chicago, observes that "whenever gang
members are in the neighborhood, even if they're just
hanging around, they intimidate the neighborhood, and
scare other kids—that's an invitation to violence."[30]

During the late 1990s in New York City, an invasion by
the Los Angeles–based Bloods renewed fears in some
neighborhoods. While tough antigang measures seemed to
be controlling the gang problem, this spread of a particularly violent gang from the West Coast set communities on
edge. *New York Daily News* columnist Stanley Crouch describes the effect of this situation on children: "Young people have enough problems adjusting to their hormones,
fighting their insecurities, trying to avoid excessive hostil-
ity toward adults. Gangs are a life-threatening extra bur-
den, and kids know it better than we do, since theirs is the
world under invasion."[31]

The movement of the Bloods into already troubled New
York City neighborhoods provoked a strong reaction. Ru-
mors began to fly that the Bloods had called for a national

initiation day and that any kids caught wearing red would be attacked. Some schools were so gripped by fear that they sent their students home. John Bess, the executive director of the Valley, a Manhattan youth agency, felt that this fear clouded the judgment of school administrators and caused them to make a poor decision. He commented, "They were sending elementary school kids outside into the street where the activity was to occur, instead of keeping them inside where they should be safe."[32]

In most cases, gang members target rival members, not just random neighborhood residents. This knowledge, however, does not calm the fears of people living in neighborhoods with a strong gang presence. They see gang

The entry of the Bloods into New York City neighborhoods has raised fears of gang violence escalating.

members assemble on street corners, often buying and selling drugs. They see threatening messages in secret code on the sides of their own apartment buildings. They hear stories about their neighbors' children getting shot on the way home from school. And they see children—some as young as eight or nine years old—associating with gang members, promising to continue the cycle of crime. Even if their own lives are not in direct danger, the fear they experience is real.

The frustration of families

To some inner-city youths, gang members appear to be the only successful people in the neighborhood. Such children and teens are attracted by the money, glamour, and prestige that gang members seem to enjoy, and parents and teachers have a hard time convincing them to stay in school and steer clear of the gang life. These young people have witnessed their neighbors who earned educations working in low-paying jobs and struggling to make ends meet; meanwhile, they see gang members who dropped out of school wearing expensive clothes and driving luxury cars. The gang way of life looks like the easy route to power and riches.

Adults in the neighborhood see a doomed generation as the children and teens around them drift into gangs and crime. Once they have been caught robbing or selling drugs, many of these young people start a downward spiral through the criminal justice system. Unless someone intervenes early enough, they often face a lifetime of repeat imprisonment, and some die early from a rival gang member's bullet.

Caught in the crossfire

The families of these young people are also victims. In neighborhoods controlled by gangs, parents often lose their children to crossfire during drug wars. Charlotte Austin, a mother who lost a son and a daughter to gang killings in Los Angeles, now speaks out about the effects of violence and organizes protest marches against gang activity in her neighborhood. She has described the fears of her one re-maining child, saying, "His fear is he's next and that's the way he's gonna die." She adds, "I'm tired of going to funer-als. I'm tired of burying nieces and cousins and brothers and nephews and children."[33]

Alicia Cabrera lives in the East New York section of Brooklyn, where fights between rival gang members—sometimes claiming the lives of innocent bystanders—are common. Her daughter, Angela Garcia, a twenty-five-year-old mother of three, was shot twice in the back and once in the head as she was leaving a party in the neighborhood. Sev-eral months after her daughter's death, Cabrera said, "I still haven't accepted that she is dead. I probably won't be able to accept it until justice is served. I can't forget she was killed, because I see her in the kids every day. I miss her so much."[34]

Unfortunately, in the case of drive-by shootings, justice often is *not* served. Those in the best position to report the details of the crime are gang members, who cover up for their fellow members and typically refuse to cooperate with the police or the courts. Other witnesses often fail to come forward as well, fearing that members of the local gang will harm them.

In addition to the families of people who are killed by gang members, the families of the gang members them-selves suffer. Families are often torn apart when a child joins a gang.

The families of gang members

For parents living in neighborhoods controlled by gangs, one of the greatest fears is that their own children will be-come gang members. Many parents warn their sons and daughters about the dangers of gang life, but they know that peer pressure is strong and they often feel helpless in the face of gangs.

When children and teens join gangs, parents often have to watch them go to juvenile detention centers or to jails. They see their children's lives being ruined as they become involved with crime and enter the juvenile justice system.

Many see their children injured in gang fights, and some even have to bury their children after they are killed by rival gang members.

The mother of a former member of the Crips recalls the shooting that cost her son his sight. Compounding her heartbreak was the lack of concern hospital personnel and the police seemed to show because her son was a gang member: "We went to the hospital, and they told me, 'Hey, he might not make it. The next two hours are crucial. He may not come out of this.' But you know what I felt like? I felt like they already believed he was going to die, because they had a toe tag on him!"[35] She comments on the response of the police: "They write in their notebook, 'Gang related,' and they leave it at that. They just go on, shrug their shoulders, and act like, well, that's the answer. It's gang related."[36]

The parents of gang members also live in fear that their other children will also be drawn into gang life. Many

A life of hopelessness and poverty often leads young people to seek escape through gang membership.

children see their older brothers or cousins take home large sums of money from selling drugs. These gang members often have fancy clothes, jewelry, and cars and may seem to command respect in the neighborhood. Younger children often idolize them, and it is hard for parents to convince these children of the dangers of gang life.

Many inner-city parents who see their children surrounded by gang members face a constant struggle to keep them from joining a gang. Poor parents recognize the temptation their children feel to make quick money and gain the protection of older gang members.

Parents struggle to keep kids out of gangs

Delbert S. Elliott, director of the Institute of Behavioral Science's Center for the Study and Prevention of Violence at the University of Colorado, Boulder, describes the frustration that many parents in gang-infested areas feel:

> The effect of living in such neighborhoods can devastate a family's attempt to provide a healthy, conventional upbringing for their children. Not only are there few social reinforcements for conventional lifestyles to support this type of parenting, but conventional opportunities are limited by racism, discrimination, social isolation from the labor market, and few resources. There are often greater opportunities for participation in gangs and the illicit economy, which offer relatively quick and substantial rewards that seem to offset the risks associated with violence. One effect of participation in these types of activities is that youth are at high risk of becoming victims as well as perpetrators of violence.[37]

One of the effects of gang violence on neighborhoods has been an increased police presence. While most residents welcome efforts to stem gang-related crime, many others feel that the show of force discriminates against minorities and interferes with their daily lives.

The presence of police

In several high-crime New York City neighborhoods with a strong gang population, an increased number of police officers now patrol the streets. This has drawn both positive and negative responses from area residents. On the one hand, it has reduced the sense of fear among many elderly people in neighborhoods where gangs have taken hold. As Michael Saliani, an eighty-eight-year-old retired piano tuner in the Bronx, comments, "We're not afraid the way we used to be. I wasn't comfortable sitting out here. My friend was robbed sitting on this stoop."[38]

Others, particularly young black and Hispanic residents, want safer streets but feel they are being unfairly targeted by the police. Twenty-four-year-old Anthony Lewis, who helps his father run a nightclub in the South Bronx, complained of being constantly questioned by officers about where he lives and why he is on the street. "They belittle you, they give you hard looks or ask, 'Why are you standing here?'" Lewis says. "You get tired of the hassles. I'm a grown man. Why can't I stand here?"[39]

Many residents of targeted neighborhoods see both sides of the issue and wish there were a better solution. They want the police to be more sensitive to the fact that the majority of inner-city residents are law-abiding citizens and to treat

Gang activity has led to an increased police presence in areas where gangs are known to recruit.

them with more respect. The Reverend Heidi Newmark of the Transfiguration Lutheran Church in the South Bronx expresses this reaction: "I have mixed feelings about the crackdown. I want drug dealers off the street. I live here, I have children. But there's a sense that the police are not on our side. There's a sense that they're here to lock us up."[40]

This makes many people living in gang-infested areas feel like prisoners in more than one way. They often hide in their apartments from the violence of gangs at war, and they also feel they must avoid police officers who suspect them of involvement in gang-related crime.

The relationship the police have with the communities where gangs live is a major factor in the way they deal with these gangs. Communities that see police officers as their allies in the struggle to control gangs tend to cooperate with police efforts. As a New York City police officer notes,

> When we get the community support, we go with it. It is so frustrating because there are some times when gang members commit a crime in the neighborhood, then we come by, but nobody is willing to help. They say they know nothing. Sometimes I don't feel like doing my job, because I know that the community is not going to cooperate in helping me get any of those who have broken the law.[41]

Most police forces try to strike a balance between using force and establishing a relationship with gangs. They try to let the gangs know that they will not tolerate violence in the community and that they will use force when necessary. However, they often overlook less serious crime in exchange for gang members' cooperation in identifying more serious offenders.

4

Cracking Down on Gang Activity

BEGINNING IN THE 1990s, police departments and the criminal justice system began to seriously crack down on gang activity. As a result, there has also been a trend toward longer prison sentences for gang members convicted of crimes. In addition to severe punishment for gang-related crime, there have been many efforts to break up gangs before they can destroy neighborhoods.

One of the more controversial ways in which the police in many cities are attempting to gain control of the gang situation is by enforcing city ordinances that discourage gang members—despite whether they have committed a crime—from assembling in the parts of town where they are known to sell drugs or commit other crimes and by imposing strict curfews. To many in communities affected by gangs, these are welcome steps. However, others feel that gang members are being unfairly singled out and that their civil liberties are being violated.

Imposing curfews and restricting assembly

Civil liberties lawyers believe that imposing curfews and curbing the freedoms of gang members is a dangerous move toward the creation of a police state. They argue that all people have the right to peaceful assembly, and restricting that right for certain groups is discrimination. Until a gang member commits a crime, they argue, he has the right to go wherever he pleases and to meet with other members of his gang. These critics are challenging local laws that limit the freedom of gangs to meet where, when, and with whom they wish. They believe that parents, and not local authorities, should decide how late their children can stay out in public and with whom they may associate.

Some critics feel that, in addition to violating young people's rights, curfews are an ineffective tool against gang crime. According to Arthur Spitzer, legal director of the American Civil Liberties Union in Washington, D.C.,

> I find it hard to believe that a curfew could have a significant effect on teenagers who are selling drugs, stealing cars or carrying a gun. The very thought that they would be deterred by a $500 fine against their parents is laughable when these kids are facing up to 10 years in the pokey. A kid won't look at the Rolex he's just stolen and say, "Oh, I've got to get home. It's 11 o'clock."[42]

However, a U.S. Department of Justice study examining the use of curfews in Chicago, Dallas, Denver, Jacksonville, New Orleans, North Little Rock, and Phoenix showed that such curfews are both legal and effective in reducing gang-related crime. The department established certain guidelines for curfew programs. These include providing a center for handling violators, with social service professionals on staff; offering counseling or referral for the families of violators; setting up fines or community

service centers for repeat offenders; providing recreation or job programs for young people; offering antidrug and antigang programs; and establishing hot lines for follow-up services.

In 1996, President Bill Clinton endorsed the right of cities to use curfews to curb gang violence, citing the Justice Department study. The president recommended that cities keep children under age eighteen off the streets after 8:00 P.M. on school nights, after 9:00 P.M. during the summer, and after 11:00 P.M. on weekends.

Legal challenges

Though curfews remain controversial, many cities with growing gang problems have adopted them. Challenges by civil libertarians have met with mixed results. In Oceanside, California, a temporary restraining order was placed on a violent street gang, Varrio Posole Locos, in 1997. It was designed to limit the activities of gang members within the gang's self-designated turf. Members were prohibited from wearing gang clothing, flashing gang signs, carrying cell phones and pagers, and publicly meeting with other gang members within that area. Legislators felt that the open display of gang symbols invited attacks by members of rival gangs and threatened public safety. The decision was challenged, but a superior court judge upheld it in March 1999.

A similar law in Chicago was successfully challenged in Illinois courts. Under the Chicago law, gang members who were found loitering in any public place and refused to leave were fined up to five hundred dollars and were sentenced for up to six months in jail. Although police officials reported that homicides dropped 26 percent after enforcement of the law, judges ruled it unconstitutional because it violated people's right to assemble.

Despite the apparent success of some curfew and anti-loitering ordinances in reducing crime, they continue to have many critics. While there is an acknowledged need to crack down on gang crime, many people are uneasy with the solution. George Brooks, director of advocacy at Kolbe House, a jail ministry, notes, "There are significant novel problems raised by gang-loitering ordinances. It is troubling when anyone can be singled out because of who they are with or the colors or symbols they are wearing."[43]

Freddy Calixto, executive director of Broader Urban Involvement and Leadership Development (BUILD), Inc., a gang violence prevention program in Chicago's West Town community, agrees: "It's a double-edged sword. We're working with young people who believe they're being harassed by law enforcement, but we're also dealing with parents who are tired of their kids being killed. We don't want a police state, but we are looking for help."[44]

Controversial antigang measures

At the same time that many cities are allowing their police forces to keep gang members from assembling, they are also encouraging them to be more aggressive in catching gang members who commit crimes. Many major cities have increased their police forces and dedicated more officers to targeting gangs. In New York City, special antigang units were created in each borough to fight gang crime. Riverside, California, has a special street-gang unit that compiles three notebooks on each targeted gang, including their arrest reports, pictures and fingerprints of members, and records of their colors, tattoos, and signs. It serves gang members notices informing them that their gang is considered a criminal organization and that participation in the gang can subject them to a one- to three-year jail sentence.

However, residents in many of these communities resist such aggressive approaches. People in cities like New York and Boston have been critical of the heavy use of force against gangs. Police officers in these cities fear charges of harassment and sometimes take a more cautious approach to gangs. Many gang members recognize this and take advantage of the opportunity it gives them to sell drugs without getting arrested. As the twenty-year-old leader of a New York City gang observes,

> Look, if we go down to peddle our wares . . . , we can make some money and not have the police on us. Check it out, remember two weeks ago when that police guy shot that young

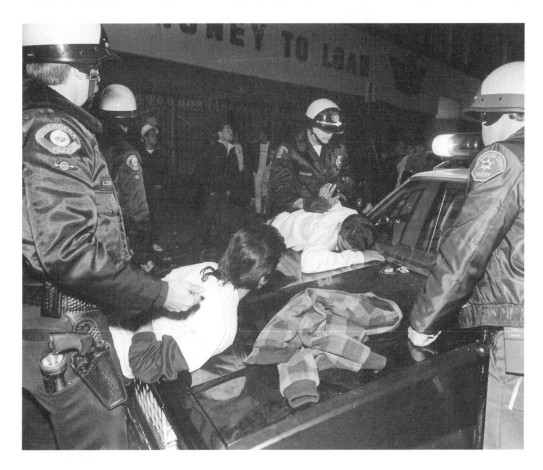

dude he thought was dealing crack? Well, now, this here is the perfect area to do business, and I say we do it, 'cause the police won't chance making another mistake or the mayor will be getting heat.[45]

Many larger cities have formed special antigang units to combat increased gang activity.

This trend toward laws that restrict gang activity is continuing at local and state levels. In addition, the federal government is hoping that antigang laws will also help to prevent crime.

The Anti-Gang and Youth Violence Control Act

In 1997, at President Clinton's urging, Congress passed the Anti-Gang and Youth Violence Control Act, a comprehensive new law designed to fight gang crime, while also supporting law enforcement efforts and the justice system. In a speech supporting the new law, Clinton stated,

The next stage in our fight must center on keeping our children safe and attacking the scourge of juvenile crime and gangs. I want every police officer, prosecutor and citizen in America working together to keep our young people safe and young criminals off the streets. This should be America's top priority in the fight for law and order over the next four years.[46]

The Anti-Gang and Youth Violence Control Act called for hiring one hundred thousand new community police officers as well as new local prosecutors. It gave local courts the authority to try juveniles as adults when they commit serious violent crimes and made it easier to release the records of juvenile criminals. To encourage witnesses of gang violence to come forward, it allowed judges to hold gang members without bail until their trials.

One of the act's goals was to curb gun violence, and it sought to prevent juveniles convicted of violent crimes from buying guns. The act increased the penalties for selling guns to minors as well as other illegal gun sales, and it set mandatory minimum sentences—requiring that all convicted offenders serve at least a certain amount of jail time—for shootings that resulted in injuries or death. It also gave police the authority to seize and destroy the guns of criminals and included measures to prevent truancy (staying out of school) and to allow curfews.

The act also served to crack down on drug sales by gangs by increasing the penalties for people who sell drugs to children, hire children to sell drugs, or sell drugs in or near schools. In addition, it gave individual states and cities the right to establish their own laws to control gang activity.

State laws against gang crime

On the state level, there have been two general approaches to creating laws to control gang crime. Some states have developed new laws that target gangs; others have amended existing laws to specifically address gang-related crimes, in some instances increasing the penalties for certain crimes commonly committed by gang members.

In Texas, the legislature proposed such measures as confiscating the cars used in drive-by shootings and suspending the driver's licenses of teens caught with guns in school. Texas representative Richard Raymond comments that "we've got to make these kids understand that it's not OK to be breaking the law, to be shooting at people, threatening people or breaking into their homes. We need to get to the point where they are afraid to break the law."[47]

Under the authority of the Anti-Gang and Youth Violence Control Act, New York state also took tougher measures against gang crime by recently enacting laws to prevent the sale of guns to minors and to keep people from hiring children or teens to market weapons. These laws were added to the Organized Crime Control Act in 1998 to make it easier for prosecutors to target gang members who

Agents from the Bureau of Alcohol, Tobacco, and Firearms display guns and other weapons confiscated during a two-day roundup of gang members in Los Angeles.

sell guns to young members or hire them as gun traffickers. The act also lets government officials seize the assets of anyone who breaks these laws. In signing the new legislation, Governor George Pataki announced, "People who sell guns to children and teenagers—or use them to traffic in illegal weapons—are among the lowest and most cowardly of all criminals. This important public safety measure will provide our law enforcement officials with an additional tool to put these despicable people out of business by seizing their ill-gotten assets."[48]

Since the passage of the Anti-Gang and Youth Violence Control Act, fourteen states have enacted new laws directed at street gangs. Some of the laws target crimes that are almost always committed by gang members, such as drive-by shootings and defacing property with graffiti. By focusing on the crime itself rather than gang membership, such laws help police and prosecutors avoid accusations that they are violating gang members' civil rights.

Five states—Florida, Georgia, Louisiana, Illinois, and California—have passed Street Terrorism Enforcement and Prevention (STEP) Acts to combat crime by gang members. These laws increase criminal penalties for people who repeatedly commit certain crimes, and they go farther than most laws in singling out gang criminals. They allow states to take away street gangs' assets and any money earned through their criminal activity, such as selling drugs.

California's STEP Act is considered a model for other states because of the way it focuses on particular crimes commonly committed by gangs. It defines seven specific crimes that, if committed more than once, show a pattern of criminal gang activity. Under the state's STEP Act, a "criminal street gang" is a group that commits one or more of these crimes and has "a common name or common identifying sign or symbol whose members individually or collectively engage in a pattern of criminal activity."[49]

Aggressive laws to prevent gang crime clearly have not come close to stopping all gang-related crime, and tough crackdowns by police departments place more gang crimi-

nals in the justice system. Just as Americans have been de-
manding more efforts toward crime prevention, they also
have been pushing for sterner penalties for offenders.

Prosecuting gang members

In a 1995 nationwide study by the National Institute of
Justice, more than 80 percent of prosecutors reported that
gangs were a problem in their jurisdiction and that they
were vigorously prosecuting crimes by gang members.
However, they also reported problems in prosecuting these
crimes because of limitations in the law.

In that study, prosecutors reported that getting the cooperation of victims and witnesses was one of their greatest
problems. Because of the power that gangs hold in many
neighborhoods, people are reluctant to speak out against
their crimes; when witnesses do come forward, they often
refuse to testify in court. These people are often threatened
by gang members if they testify, or they may be gang
members themselves and refuse to turn against their own
group out of loyalty or fear. Prosecutors point to a need for
more funding for witness protection programs—which
protect the identity of people who testify against violent
criminals, and for victim advocates—people who prepare
victims for trial and reassure them of their safety. They
also reported in the 1995 study being particularly frus-
trated by problems in trying cases against juveniles because state juvenile laws were not designed to address the
serious violence of much street-gang crime.

Since the enactment of the Anti-Gang and Youth Violence Control Act, however, the courts have been granted
permission to take stronger measures against gang members. The act allows judges to consider membership in a
street gang when setting bail—the amount of money de-
fendants must pay to stay out of jail until their case goes to
trial. Higher bail means that more gang members, many of
whom actually have little money, go to jail as soon as they
are arrested.

The violence of gangs can now be considered a special
factor, and their crimes are treated as extreme threats to

society. Public reaction to gang violence led the courts to expand the list of serious crimes for which minors can be tried as adults to include certain gun and drug offenses as well as crimes of conspiracy (in which members of a group plan the crime together).

Prosecuting juveniles as adults

In many states there is a trend toward lowering the age at which juveniles may be tried as adults for serious crimes. In recent years, the Massachusetts House of Representatives voted to require accused murderers as young as fourteen years old to be tried as adults. Tennessee eliminated any minimum age, Oregon lowered its minimum age from fourteen to twelve, and Wisconsin lowered it to ten. In Oklahoma, sixteen- and seventeen-year-olds who commit certain violent crimes must convince the court why they should not be tried as adults. Consequently, juvenile gang members are also more likely than other minors to be tried as adults for their crimes.

A dilemma the courts face is whether to prosecute teenage gang members as juveniles or adults.

In trying a juvenile as an adult, the court is seeking a longer jail sentence. However, juveniles convicted as adults remain in juvenile detention centers until they turn eighteen. They may be moved to an adult facility at age sixteen, but only if they are considered a danger to other inmates.

Another reason why many people want violent juveniles to be tried as adults is to make their criminal records public. Since the courts seal juvenile records, their criminal histories are hidden even from lawyers prosecuting them for later crimes. As Ed Koch, the former mayor of New York City and a practicing judge, notes,

> In our zeal to protect the privacy of young thugs, we've established a system where convicted juvenile criminals can't be identified to the public. Juveniles engage in crime because there is no respect for law or authority and little expectation of arrest or punishment. Our state legislators fail to recognize that the crimes committed by these "little rascals" have gone way beyond pickpocketing, slashing tires and drinking beer in public. The laws created to handle those misdemeanors are simply not adequate to deal with the serious felonies that juveniles are now committing.[50]

Special gang units

Just as special police units have been making their presence known in neighborhoods with high rates of gang-related crime, in many states special gang units are making bold statements within the court system. In Denver, the district attorney's office established its gang unit in the late 1980s to address the growing problem of gang-related crime in that city. The unit works closely with other law enforcement agencies on the federal, state, and local levels to coordinate investigations and gather information and evidence to prosecute gang members. The gang unit has succeeded in convicting some of the highest-ranking gang leaders in Denver.

The hard line that the courts are now taking to prevent gang violence reflects the public's fear and anger toward gang criminals. However, prosecutors face many challenges in their cases against gang members. Although people insist

Members of the Detroit Police Gang Squad assist with an arrest.

that the courts crack down on illegal gang activity, only individual gang members can be prosecuted, and many critics believe that this has little if any effect in decreasing gang crime.

Gang members themselves are aware of how little impact these cases have on their activity. As a sixteen-year-old member of a Los Angeles gang notes,

> I gone to court about three times now to see some of the brothers get tried. And each time I went, the judge said he was going to get tough with gangs because they were a social threat to society. Then he said he was going to give the brothers a long sentence because they were leaders and he wanted to take the lifeblood out of the gang. . . . I just laughed, 'cause there is no way that sending anybody to prison can kill a gang.[51]

Sentencing for gang-related crimes

Public anger at the violence of gang members has pressured legislators to push for tougher sentencing. As a result, many judges are imposing maximum sentences on gang members convicted of violent killings, in part to set an example for other gang members or those thinking about joining gangs. More and more minors who commit serious crimes are being sentenced as adults and spending many years behind bars. Some are transferred from juvenile to adult facilities as soon as they are old enough. A few gang members have even received the death penalty for committing particularly brutal crimes, with their history of gang violence considered a special factor.

In 1997 nineteen-year-old Michael Boreta of Texas was sentenced to twenty years in prison—the maximum term possible—for the fatal stabbing of a member of a rival street gang. A condition of the sentence was that he must serve at least half of it before he is eligible for parole. In requesting the long sentence, assistant criminal defense attorney Frank Webb said that a harsh decision was needed to discourage other young people from joining gangs. He said of Boreta, "Will his 12-year-old brother say, 'That's what I want to do [commit murder]. I want to do the same thing'? And will he do the same thing or will he be on the receiving end?"[52]

In Los Angeles, where street-gang crime has been a major problem for many years, the law takes a hard line in sentencing and states that,

> If it is established that a person is a gang member (e.g., through affiliation, clothing, witness testimony), the policy is to seek the maximum penalty. Pursuit of the maximum penalty is guided by the belief that gang members commit a greater variety of crimes than non-gang members; gang members commit crimes over a longer period of time than non-gang members; gang members are more violent than non-gang members.[53]

Gang members in prison

As a result of tough sentencing, there are a lot of gang members in the American prison population, and gangs have become a major part of the prison culture. They often pressure other inmates to join their gangs, and many prisoners do join for protection while in jail.

Because of tough antigang laws, there has been an increase of gang members in America's prison population.

Because of the problems that gang members create in prisons, many of the more violent ones are segregated from other prisoners. In a 1998 series on gang members in prison, ABC News reporter Ted Koppel noted,

> If prison intelligence confirms an inmate's membership in one of these gangs, the prisoner is automatically transferred out of the general population to the administrative segregation unit. If he's already a member when he's sentenced, he will spend his entire sentence in solitary. An inmate could return to the general prison population if he renounced his membership in the gang. But then he would probably be killed. He has to shed blood to be accepted in the first place, and membership is considered a lifetime affair.[54]

A member of a Chicago gang, the Vice Lords, expresses the frustration of many gang members in prison. Albert McGee, who is serving a sentence for homicide and drug possession at Mississippi State Penitentiary, observes, "It doesn't matter how much good I do. The fact that I'm a known gang member is enough. Forget that I'm going to college here. Forget that I've not had a violation report since I came here in '90. They look for the wrong in me, just because I'm a known gang member."[55]

To some observers, gang members are not only given harsher sentences because of their membership but are also singled out for greater confinement in prison. Others find, however, that isolating violent criminals who are a danger to the rest of the prison population is necessary. They also wish to prevent gang members from influencing other inmates to join their gang. Some further argue that isolation is for the gang members' own protection from attacks by rivals.

Many people fear that prison actually helps strengthen gang membership and loyalty and reinforces members' antisocial ways of thinking. Virginia Poole, the mother of a young skinhead who is serving a twenty-year sentence for burglary, believes that prison is making her son more violent and full of hate. For twenty-three hours each day, he is in solitary confinement in a windowless cell. Poole observes, "No mother's child should be living like this. Sometimes instead of our system making better people out of them, it makes them worse, and that hurts and everybody loses."[56]

Alternatives to prison

There is a common concern that throwing young people in jail for many years will only create hardened criminals who will commit worse crimes after their release. Some people believe that rescuing them when they are still young will save lives later. Young gang members, they argue, are much more impressionable and open to rehabilitation than older ones who have committed a string of crimes and spent many years in prison.

As a result, some courts have been trying new alternatives to imprisoning young offenders. In Spokane, Washington, juvenile court administrator Tom Davis used a fifty-seven thousand dollar federal grant to turn a garage below a detention center into a schoolroom for twenty teen offenders. Davis's innovative project combines day detention with community service, encouraging young offenders to become contributing members of the community. During the day, the teens attend classes and perform community service in their neighborhood. At night, they wear electronic monitors on their ankles to ensure that they do not leave their homes.

One participant in the program, Luke Riddle, was a sixteen-year-old member of a skinhead gang when he was arrested for attempted assault and reckless endangerment of a black teen. Following the completion of his sentence at Davis's day facility, Riddle claimed that the combination of individual attention in school, counseling, and reconnection with his family helped him quit the gang, reject his racist views, and look toward a productive future. Riddle notes, "I don't think sitting in a jail cell would've done me any good. I would've come out 10 times worse." His mother observed, "I just thank God we were where they had this program. I don't think he would've had a chance without it."[57]

The success of the Spokane program encouraged juvenile court administrators to try similar projects in other counties. However, such programs are equipped to deal only with relatively minor offenders. Once a gang member has killed or committed another serious crime, he is likely to spend many years of his life behind bars.

5

Preventing Gang-Related Crime

ALTHOUGH MANY PEOPLE support efforts by the police and the courts to rid their communities of gang-related crime, most agree that such efforts will not entirely solve the problems posed by gangs. Most jailed gang members are eventually back on the streets, committing more crimes and recruiting new members. In fact, many people join gangs while in prison. As long as gang life continues to appeal to young people, they will continue to join gangs and cause problems in their neighborhoods. The best remedy for gang-related crime, nearly all experts agree, is prevention.

Organizations to prevent gang activity

A wide variety of organizations work to prevent people from joining gangs and to encourage current gang members to quit. These range from grassroots groups that organize within neighborhoods to organizations run by the federal government.

At the local level, concerned parents often organize to alert others in the community of the dangers of gang violence. They hold rallies to protest gang activity in their neighborhoods and pressure politicians to pass tough anti-gang laws, such as laws that require long prison sentences for the types of crimes gang members tend to commit. They may closely follow court cases involving gang members to let them know that they cannot get away with their

Many neighborhoods have united in their efforts to combat gang violence. Here, Detroit's "Neighborhoods Against Gangs" holds a prayer meeting to protest gangs.

crimes. Many proponents believe that this type of community activism is an effective tool in the fight against criminal gang activity. By showing that they care about what happens in the neighborhood, residents send a signal to gang members to keep out. They also make it less attractive for kids to join gangs since they know their activity will be closely monitored.

Private and government-run agencies also play a major role in deterring gang crime. Organizations like the National Youth Gang Project, which was founded in 1987, study which programs and policies are most effective in preventing people from joining gangs and in reforming gang members. The project is run by the Office of Juvenile Justice and Delinquency Prevention, which assists communities in responding to gangs. Some local organizations, such as Youth Guidance in Chicago, are run by church groups and focus on helping poor inner-city youths through counseling, education, and job development and training.

Other groups are operated by law enforcement agencies and use the threat of punishment to discourage gang activity.

One of these groups is Streetworkers, a Boston organization that warns young people about the consequences of gang crime. Hewett Joyner, a member of the group, notes,

> Our job is to go out there and tell the boys—or the girls—on the block, this is gettin' ready to happen to you. If you don't pay attention and stop the shootings, the stabbings, the beat-downs, then the Feds are gonna come get you, and this is no joke, man. When the Feds come out, there's nothing we can do. So they're trying to give us a chance to work with you be-fore you end up in federal prison.[58]

The court system is also involved in trying to prevent gang activity. The Denver district attorney's gang unit works with the police department to create awareness in the community to show gangs that their crimes will not be tolerated. It offers seminars and organizes neighborhood programs to control gang activities and promote safer streets.

In 1996, U.S. attorney general Janet Reno announced her support for both prevention measures and strong prose-cution of gang crime. She stated that law enforcement is "committed to putting these gangs out of business—with a tough, smart mix of prosecutions, police, aid to communi-ties and common-sense programs to invest in young people before they take the wrong path. And we will support com-munity innovations like school uniforms, curfews and tru-ancy prevention."[59]

While there are different opinions on which approach is most effective, experts agree that education is a key ele-ment in keeping kids from joining gangs. Learning that there is a high price to pay for belonging to a gang—and that there are positive alternatives—is enough to steer some kids away from gang membership.

Educating young people about gangs

Because the lure of gangs can be powerful to children and teens in poor urban neighborhoods, educators stress the importance of exposing the negative side of gang life. Many young people see only the money, power, and glamour of belonging to a gang and do not recognize that joining a gang often leads to a cycle of violence and jail time, and sometimes even early death.

One of the most effective ways of showing children the harm that gangs cause communities and their members is by having former gang members talk about their experiences. Young people who are rebelling against parents, teachers, and other authority figures are more likely to listen to those who have tried the gang life and experienced firsthand the damage it causes. Many educational programs recruit former gang members who have committed crimes, spent time in jail, and then learned from their mistakes. These men and women are in the best position to describe what gang life is really like and how grateful they are to have a second chance at leading a productive life.

Julius Nicholson, an eighteen-year-old former gang member, now works with the Metro Detroit Girls and Boys Club, where he offers counseling and support for neighborhood kids. One of the boys who he is helping to break free of gang life once followed him into crime. Nicholson

Some former gang members now lecture children about the dangers of joining gangs.

recalls, "I asked him why he did it, and he said because he saw me doing it. I felt bad, because I didn't know I was leading him."[60] Nicholson now has an opportunity to be a positive, rather than negative, role model.

The Gang Resistance Education and Training (GREAT) program is a government-sponsored program run by the federal Bureau of Alcohol, Tobacco, and Firearms (ATF) to educate schoolchildren about gangs. This program was developed in 1992 in Phoenix, Arizona, to address an increasing youth gang problem in that city. It now operates in classrooms in forty-five states and Washington, D.C., as well as at U.S. military bases overseas. Today, approximately 13,000 officers from more than 530 agencies have been trained to teach schoolchildren about the dangers of gang life and how to resolve conflict without using violence. More than 2 million American children have graduated from the GREAT program. While its main focus is on teens, GREAT offers programs for grades three through six as well as a summer recreation program.

In the GREAT program, trained officers teach children how to set and meet goals on the road to becoming responsible citizens. The officers help students learn various life skills to combat violence, prejudice, victimization, and negative attitudes toward law enforcement. The program shows students how crime destroys their neighborhoods and encourages them to work together to solve problems without resorting to violence. It also focuses on ways students can meet their needs without joining gangs. GREAT gets kids involved in helping their communities with projects like painting over graffiti and doing volunteer work for neighborhood programs. When children feel they have a stake in the community, they are less likely to commit destructive acts against it.

A similar program in California is CHOICES, which focuses on at-risk middle-school students in San Bernardino and Orange Counties. The program's goal is to reduce drug use, failure in school, gang membership, and crime. Like GREAT, CHOICES seeks to improve neighborhoods by involving students in the community. Participants in

CHOICES take a seventeen-week class taught by police officers, attend a youth wilderness camp, and attend an after-care or follow-up program. Students focus on learning to work together, solving problems, and role-playing, and they learn self-control and decision-making skills.

There are many other programs throughout the country that use education to keep young people from joining gangs and convincing those already in gangs to quit. All seek to show kids constructive rather than destructive ways of living.

While most people applaud programs that educate students about gangs, some feel that it is not enough. They argue that though many kids respond well to the positive attention and guidance, others will continue to join gangs and commit crimes. They believe that the only way to prevent these gang members from destroying their communities is to keep them off the streets.

Rico Rush (center), from the Alliance of Concerned Men, hugs former gang member Eric Reavis (right) following a truce agreement between two rival gangs in Washington, D.C.

Programs to provide alternatives

Job opportunities and the promise of a better future are essential to discouraging young people from joining gangs. As criminologist and filmmaker Roger Graef, who spent six years researching youth gangs, notes, "The crucial part of the argument about guns and crime and drugs is that saying no is not enough, they need something to say yes to. They need to have a sense of the future that is beyond the weekend. They need to see that they will get the kind of rewards, financially, emotionally, and professionally, that hard work really delivers."[61]

This need to provide positive alternatives to drugs and crime is being recognized by many legislators. In a 1997 statement to Congress introducing new legislation to fight youth violence, Senator Joseph R. Biden said,

> It seems to me that we do know at least one thing about preventing youth crime and drug abuse—we need to get kids off the streets and into supervised programs during the after-school hours when kids are likely to be the victims of gangs and gang criminals or the "customers" of drug pushers. If we can just do that simple thing, with Boys & Girls Clubs or many other proven efforts, we can make important in-roads against drug abuse and crime among children.[62]

Many cities that have gang problems have programs in place to provide counseling and recreational activities for young gang members and those at risk of joining gangs. These government-sponsored programs help kids channel their energy into constructive activities, teaching them new skills and creating an environment of cooperation. They teach them to value and respect others, including their former gang rivals.

In Austin, Texas, the Roving Leader program is a non-profit organization that targets those between the ages of nine and nineteen at risk of gang involvement. It offers youth and parent support groups on school campuses as well as after-school and evening programs such as tutoring, cooking classes, and recreational activities. The program encourages students to finish high school and helps them set goals and make responsible choices

In Dallas, Nuestro Centro ("Our Center") is a gang and drug intervention program that offers counseling, parenting classes, tutoring, educational field trips, and high school and college courses. The program uses peer pressure and interaction to help kids communicate rather than act out through violence. Nuestro Centro assigns a volunteer mentor to each youth for one year, with whom he or she meets weekly. This offers a positive role model and a strong support system and helps identify problems not apparent in groups. Each week role model speakers give presentations on reaching goals, educational and career opportunities, work skills, and the dangers of drugs. SAT and GED preparation programs are also available to encourage teens to pursue a higher education. Parenting courses help teach parents of at-risk youths effective skills to increase communication with their children.

In Pierce County, Washington, Safe Streets is a community resource to help young people, their families, and communities reduce gang violence and drug use. Among its programs are an interagency task force to unite schools, health services, the police department, the prosecuting attorney's office, and the department of children's services to identify gang members and break the cycle of violence. Programs for young people include Joining with Schools, in which five thousand students ages twelve to eighteen examine the choices they make with adult mentors; after-school sports programs, which are supplemented by programs in conflict resolution, self-discipline, teambuilding, and intercultural understanding; Positive Alternatives, a program that addresses drug and alcohol use, physical abuse, gang activities, and family problems; and employment programs that provide job training.

In addition to programs directed at preventing gang activity, there are many community organizations that can help serve kids' needs for group companionship and support. Roger Quintana, crime prevention specialist for the Boise School District and a former police officer, urges parents to get involved in these organizations, noting, "For every negative gang, the percentage of good gangs is greater. There's YMCA, Boys and Girls Clubs, Boy Scouts, athletics, parks and recreation, Little League, band. Kids need to belong in a good way."[63]

Unfortunately, many young people fail to get involved with prevention programs soon enough. For others, such programs are not enough to fight the temptation to join a gang. Once kids have become gang members, the battle to free them from a life of crime and punishment is harder.

Rehabilitating gang members

Many programs focus on rehabilitating gang members so that they can reenter society as productive citizens. In Los Angeles, one innovative program pairs convicted criminals with disabled students. By helping these students with special needs, the former gang members learn work skills, connect with others in a positive way, and develop self-esteem. The program has been copied in Little Rock, Arkansas, a city that has also developed serious gang problems.

Steve Nawojczyk, a former Arkansas coroner who has studied street gangs since 1987, cites this program and others as better solutions than jail. "Their heroes are in jail," he notes. "We have to come up with better solutions. Maybe some of the punishments we're using aren't working." Speaking to a group of educators, law enforcement officers, and clergy as part of "Making Our Schools Safe," a conference sponsored by the Massachusetts Teachers Association, Nawojczyk stressed the importance of listening to young gang members and understanding their frustrations: "We must hear them. We must know why they're forming their own societies, why they feel like failures in ours."[64]

Other efforts at preventing gang activity

Many people recognize that education and special programs are not always enough to keep kids from being lured into gangs. While most programs aim at providing positive alternatives, some experts insist that certain prohibitions are also necessary.

Some communities are trying to keep kids off the streets by extending school hours and lengthening the school year.

In an effort to reduce gang violence, many schools have banned certain clothing and hairstyles. Here, seventh-grader Torie Nicholas (right) speaks out against this policy at her school.

They believe that by spending more time in school, young people will have less opportunity to form gangs and develop rivalries. Some schools are requiring that students wear uniforms in an effort to prevent them from wearing gang clothing. Community and school leaders are also removing gang graffiti immediately to show that it will not be tolerated. Likewise, many inner-city schools are using metal detectors to keep gang members from bringing in guns, knives, and other weapons.

Many of the people who promote these efforts believe that American society has allowed kids too many personal freedoms and that young people secretly want more structure and discipline. They see antisocial behavior as a way of asking for help. As Mike Knox, a fifteen-year veteran of the Houston Police Department and one of the founders of its Westside Command Divisional Gang Unit, asserts,

> The solutions to crime problems are being screamed at us by our young people: firm, fair, and consistent discipline. . . . I know that gang members respond to discipline; evidence can be obtained by interviewing any boot camp counselor or ad-

ministrator, who will report great success with some of the most hardcore gang members. The reason: the military environment is, in many ways, a parallel of the gang life from which they come. They understand, almost intuitively, the need to obey the commands of a superior.[65]

Another police officer, Sergeant Peter Ritter, supervisor of the Gang Investigation Unit for the Boise Police Department, agrees that young people need more restrictions: "I see a lot of kids who are in trouble. The big recurring theme is that nobody has set limits. Kids don't feel comfortable if they don't know what the limits are."[66]

An ongoing struggle

Today, many people are working toward both addressing the problems that lead young people to join gangs and keeping gang members from taking over the streets of America's cities. Parents, teachers, clergy, the police, lawyers, judges, legislators, parole officers, and counselors are all trying to save the next generation of American youth from needlessly embarking on a road toward crime, punishment, and even death.

Greg Boyle, a Jesuit priest at Dolores Mission Church in East Los Angeles, sums up the situation well: "We're dealing with an enormously complex social ill that must be addressed on many fronts such as poverty, despair, boredom, unemployment and failure of schools. Although law enforcement plays an important role, the police cannot address root causes."[67]

This situation was first recognized as a crisis during the 1980s, and American society continues to struggle to find effective solutions. Most experts acknowledge that no single solution works. They recognize that society needs to change before American youth will stop joining gangs. The roots of gang activity—poverty, discrimination, poor education, and the breakdown of families—need to be addressed. These problems have always existed and cannot be solved quickly.

Notes

Chapter 1: The Appeal of Gangs

1. Quoted in Sandra Gardner, *Street Gangs in America.* New York: Franklin Watts, 1992, p. 64.

2. Quoted in Martin Sanchez Jankowski, *Islands in the Street: Gangs and American Urban Society.* Berkeley and Los Angeles: University of California Press, 1991, p. 305.

3. Quoted in Judy Grigg Hansen, "Gang Prevention," *Boise Family Magazine,* May 1997. http://family.go.com/ Features/family_1997_05/bois/bois57gang/bois57gang.html.

4. Gardner, *Street Gangs in America,* p. 11.

5. Quoted in Jankowski, *Islands in the Street,* p. 47.

6. Quoted in Gail B. Stewart, *The Other America: Gangs.* San Diego: Lucent Books, 1997, p. 54.

7. Laron Douglas, "In the Mind of a True Disciple," *Prison Life,* March 1995.

8. Alan McEvoy, Edsel Erickson, and Norman Randolph, "Why the Brutality?" Urban Education Web. http://eric-web.tc.columbia.edu/administration/safety/gang_brutality.

9. Quoted in Stewart, *The Other America: Gangs,* p. 84.

10. Quoted in Jankowski, *Islands in the Street,* p. 42.

11. Quoted in PBS Online, *In Search of Law and Order: Reclaiming America's Kids,* part 1. www.pbs.org/lawand order/files/transcript1.txt.

12. Quoted in Kim Curtis, "Death Row Advice: Say No to Gangs," *San Diego Union-Tribune,* February 21, 1999, p. A-23.

13. Quoted in Curtis, "Death Row Advice," p. A-23.

14. Quoted in PBS Online, *In Search of Law and Order: Reclaiming America's Kids*, part 3. www.pbs.org/lawand order/files/transcript3.txt.

15. Quoted in Randi Henderson, "Caught in the Crossfire," *Common Boundary,* January/February 1995.

16. Quoted in Jankowski, *Islands in the Street*, p. 45.

Chapter 2: Gangs, Drugs, and Violence

17. Federal Bureau of Investigation, "Gang Alert." www.fbi.gov/kids/crimepre/gang.gang.htm.

18. Quoted in PBS Online, *In Search of Law and Order*, part 1.

19. Quoted in Jankowski, *Islands in the Street*, p. 81.

20. Douglas, "In the Mind of a True Disciple."

21. Patrick Leahy, "Democratic Youth Violence, Crime, and Drug Abuse Bill," January 15, 1997. www.senate.gov/~leahy/e.html.

22. Quoted in Steve Macko, "Street Gang Franchises, Exporting Drugs," EmergencyNet News Service, January 21, 1996. www. emergency.com/gangfran.htm.

23. Quoted in McEvoy, Edsel, and Randolph, "Why the Brutality?"

24. Quoted in Melanie McFarland, "Kids Under the Gun: KCTS-TV's 'Cease Fire' Looks at the Deadly Interplay of Teens and Firearms," *Seattle Times,* October 28, 1997. www.seattletimes.com/extra/browser/html/97/fire_102897.html.

25. Quoted in Educational Fund to End Handgun Violence, *Kids and Guns: A National Disgrace,* 3rd ed. Washington, DC: Educational Fund to End Handgun Violence, 1993.

26. Elijah Anderson, "The Code of the Streets," *The Atlantic Monthly,* 273, no. 5, May 1994.

Chapter 3: Life in a Gang-Infested Neighborhood

27. Quoted in PBS Online, *In Search of Law and Order*, part 1.

28. Quoted in Jankowski, *Islands in the Street,* p. 200.

29. Quoted in Stewart, *The Other America: Gangs,* pp. 20–21.

30. Quoted in Rebecca Leung, "Taking Back the Community," ABCNews.com, December 2, 1998. www.abcnews.go.com/sections/us/DailyNews/gangloitering981202.html.

31. Stanley Crouch, "Bloods Are Our Local Terrorists," *New York Daily News,* October 8, 1997. www.nydailynews.com/archive/97.

32. Quoted in E. K. Shipp, "Nabes Can Slash Gang Activity," *New York Daily News,* October 28, 1997. www.nydaily news.com/archive.

33. Quoted in Anne McDermott, "Fighting Fear in the Face of Gang Violence," CNN Interactive, August 22, 1996. http://cnn.com/us9608/22/charlotte.loss/index.html.

34. Quoted in Michele McPhee and Jorge Fitz-Gibbon, "Some Streets Still Killing Fields," *New York Daily News,* December 31, 1998. www.nydailynews.com/1998-12-31/ News_and_Views/crime/file/a-15194.asp.

35. Quoted in Stewart, *The Other America: Gangs,* pp. 72–73.

36. Quoted in Stewart, *The Other America: Gangs,* pp. 74–75.

37. Delbert S. Elliott, "Youth Violence: An Overview," University of Pennsylvania, Philadelphia, Center for the Study of Youth Policy, 1993.

38. Quoted in Paul Schwartzman, "NYPD Takes Back Streets," *New York Daily News,* May 20, 1998.

39. Quoted in Schwartzman, "NYPD Takes Back Streets."

40. Quoted in Schwartzman, "NYPD Takes Back Streets."

41. Quoted in Jankowski, *Islands in the Street,* p. 256.

Chapter 4: Cracking Down on Gang Activity

42. Quoted in Craig Donegan, "Preventing Juvenile Crime," *CQ Researcher,* March 15, 1996.

43. George Brooks, "Let's Not Gang Up on Our Kids," *U.S. Catholic,* March 1997.

44. Quoted in Leung, "Taking Back the Community."

45. Quoted in Jankowski, *Islands in the Street,* p. 255.

46. Quoted in U.S. Department of Justice, "The President's Anti-Gang and Youth Violence Strategy." www.usdoj.gov/ ag/anti-gang.htm.

47. Quoted in Anna M. Tinsley, "State Lawmakers Taking Steps to Crack Down on Gang Violence," *Texas News,* January 2, 1997. www.texnews.com/news/gangs010297.html.

48. Quoted in "Governor Pataki Targets Gun Traffickers Who Use Children" (press release), August 20, 1998. www.state.ny.us/governor/press/aug20_1_98.htm.

49. Claire Johnson, Barbara Webster, and Edward Connors, "Prosecuting Gangs: A National Assessment," National Insti-

tute of Justice Research in Brief, February 1995. www.ncjrs.
org/txtfiles/pgang.txt.

50. Ed Koch, "Get Control of Juvenile Terrorists," *American Enterprise,* May/June 1995.

51. Quoted in Jankowski, *Islands in the Street,* p. 268.

52. Quoted in *Lubbock Avalanche-Journal,* "Man Receives Twenty-Year Term in Shooting Death," May 23, 1997. www.lubbockonline.com/news/052397/man.htm.

53. Quoted in National Institute of Justice, NIJ Research in Brief, "Prosecuting Gangs: A National Assessment," February 1995. www.ncjrs.org/txtfiles/pgang.txt.

54. Quoted in ABC News, "Crime and Punishment," *Nightline,* March 27, 1998. http://archive.abcnews.go.com/sections/us/DailyNews/n10327_prisons.html.

55. Albert McGee, "Ridin' Under the Five-Pointed Star," *Prison Life,* March 1995.

56. Quoted in ABC News, "Crime and Punishment."

57. Quoted in Susan Byrnes, "New Program a Lifesaver, Youth Says," *Seattle Times,* August 30, 1996. www.seattletimes.com/extra/browse/htm/luke_083096.html.

Chapter 5: Preventing Gang-Related Crime

58. Quoted in PBS Online, *In Search of Law and Order,* part 1.

59. Quoted in Steve Macko, "Nationwide Survey Shows Gang Problems Getting Worse," EmergencyNet News Service, June 22, 1996. www.emergency.com/doj-gang.htm.

60. Quoted in Ann Curran, "Detroit Club Helps Kids Kick Habit," CNN Interactive, August 14, 1996. http://cnn.com/US/9608/14/kid.crime.avoidance/index.html.

61. Quoted in PBS Online, *In Search of Law and Order,* part 1.

62. Democratic Leadership Committee, "Statement of Senator Joseph R. Biden: Introduction of Crime, Youth Violence, and Drug Abuse Legislation," January 15, 1997. www. senate.gov/~dpc/events/970115/biden.html.

63. Quoted in Hansen, "Gang Prevention."

64. Quoted in Stephanie McLaughlin, "Ex-Coroner Aims

to Build Awareness of Gangs," *Boston Globe,* March 12, 1995. www.gangwar.com/news05.htm.

65. Mike Knox, *Gangsta in the House: Understanding Gang Culture.* Troy, MI: Momentum Books, 1995, p. 176.

66. Quoted in Hansen, "Gang Prevention."

67. Greg Boyle, "Gang Life," *Spirituality,* Spring 1994.

Organizations to Contact

Boston Violence Youth Prevention Program (BVYPP)
1010 Massachusetts Ave.
Boston, MA 02118
(617) 534-5196

The BVYPP teaches violence prevention strategies to counselors and trainers, who then work with public schools and community centers. It sponsors gang and drug prevention programs and publishes a bimonthly newsletter.

California Youth Authority Gang Violence Reduction Project
2445 N. Mariondale Ave.
Los Angeles, CA 90032
(213) 227-4114

This project, operated by California parole agents, tries to mediate feuds among gangs in East Los Angeles. It develops job opportunities for former gang members, removes gang graffiti, and establishes parent groups. Members speak to organizations about gang prevention and related topics. The project publishes pamphlets and a directory of organizations concerned with gangs.

Community Organizations United to Reduce the Area's Gang Environment (Project COURAGE)
Riverside County Office of Education
3939 13th St.
Riverside, CA 92502
(909) 369-7860

Project COURAGE, for grades K–8, provides youth with positive alternatives to gang membership and substance abuse. The project works to improve students' stability, empowerment, self-esteem, and educational commitment.

Gang Resistance Education and Training (GREAT)

GREAT Branch
PO Box 50418
Washington, DC 20091
(800) 726-7070

This model program for grades K–12 has resulted in lower rates of delinquency and gang affiliation and in more negative attitudes about gangs.

Gang Risk Intervention Program (GRIP)

Safe Schools and Violence Prevention Office
California Department of Education
560 J St.
Sacramento, CA 95814
(916) 323-1026

A model program for middle and high schools, GRIP was first instituted in the Los Angeles area and now operates in fifteen California counties. Its major goals are to tie youth to community organizations and to commit businesses and community groups to providing positive youth activities.

National Council on Crime and Delinquency

685 Market St.
San Francisco, CA 94105
(415) 896-6223

This organization supports crime prevention programs aimed at strengthening families, reducing school-dropout rates, and increasing employment opportunities for disadvantaged youth. It publishes journals, research briefs, and policy papers.

National Crime Prevention Council (NCPC)

1700 K St. NW
Washington, DC 20006-3817
(202) 466-6272

The NCPC provides training and technical assistance to those interested in crime prevention. It promotes job training and recreational programs as a means of reducing youth crime and violence. The council publishes a book, a booklet, and newsletters, and it sponsors the Take a Bite Out of Crime campaign.

National Institute of Justice (NIJ)
PO Box 6000
Rockville, MD 20849-6000
(800) 851-3420

The NIJ is the federal government's primary sponsor of research on crime and its control. It sponsors research efforts through grants and contracts that are carried out by universities, private institutions, and state and local agencies, and produces several publications.

Youth Crime Watch of America (YCWA)
9300 S. Dadeland Blvd.
Miami, FL 33156
(305) 670-3805

This nonprofit student-led organization promotes crime and drug prevention programs in communities and schools throughout the country. Member-students help raise public awareness concerning alcohol and drug abuse, crime, gangs, guns, and the importance of education. The YCWA publishes a quarterly newsletter.

Suggestions for Further Reading

S. Beth Atkin, *Voices from the Street: Young Gang Members Tell Their Stories.* Boston: Little, Brown, 1996. This book includes interviews with former gang members from different parts of the United States, with their photographs and poems.

Sandra Gardner, *Street Gangs in America.* New York: Franklin Watts, 1992. A writer on youth and family issues for the *New York Times* examines the reasons young people are drawn to gangs and how gang membership affects them, their families, and society.

Joyce Carol Oates, *Foxfire: Confessions of a Girl Gang.* New York: Plume Books, 1994. In this novel, the award-winning author explores the lives of five alienated teenage girls who form a gang and get caught up in violence.

Deborah Prothrow-Stith, *Deadly Consequences: How Violence Is Destroying Our Teenage Population and a Plan to Begin Solving the Problem.* New York: HarperCollins, 1998. This book, by a former Massachusetts commissioner of public health, explores the epidemic of violence among young men living in poverty and suggests solutions. The author recommends a public awareness campaign like the one aimed at preventing people from smoking as well as increased funding for mental health agencies and an antiviolence curriculum in schools.

Gini Sikes, *Eight Ball Chicks: A Year in the Violent World of Girl Gangs.* New York: Anchor Books, 1992. The author of this book spent almost two years in Los Angeles, San

Antonio, and Milwaukee following three girls' gangs and exploring their lives. The book offers firsthand accounts of these girls' experiences and stresses the factors that drove them to join gangs: fear and the desperate desire for safety and status in the inner city.

Gail B. Stewart, *The Other America: Gangs.* San Diego: Lucent Books, 1997. This illustrated book presents interviews with young gang members to give readers an inside look into why they join and how they see their roles within the gang and society.

James Diego Vigil, *Barrio Gangs: Street Life and Identity in Southern California.* Austin: University of Texas Press, 1988. In this book, the author draws on his experiences as a youth worker, high-school teacher, and researcher in the barrios of Southern California. He interviews Latino gang members and focuses on their reasons for joining gangs, including isolation from mainstream American culture, poverty, family stress and overcrowded living conditions, peer pressure, and the adolescent struggle for self-identity.

Works Consulted

Books

Charles P. Cozic, ed., *Opposing Viewpoints: Gangs.* San Diego: Greenhaven, 1996. One of a series of books that presents debates on social issues, *Gangs* offers the views of both experts in the field and gang members on how gangs affect American society. The essays are preceded with questions that encourage the readers to consider various viewpoints.

Mike Knox, *Gangsta in the House: Understanding Gang Culture.* Troy, MI: Momentum Books, 1995. A veteran of the Houston Police Department discusses how American society may be encouraging gang behavior and presents ideas for preventing young people from joining gangs.

A. E. Sadler, ed., *Opposing Viewpoints: Juvenile Crime.* San Diego: Greenhaven, 1997. This volume in the Opposing Viewpoints series examines the ideas of educators, law enforcement officials, and others on the causes of juvenile crime, including crime by gang members, and ways to combat it.

Martin Sanchez Jankowski, *Islands in the Street: Gangs and American Urban Society.* Berkeley and Los Angeles: University of California Press, 1991. In this book, a sociology professor at the University of California, Berkeley, examines the organization of gangs and the role they play in American society.

Periodicals

Elijah Anderson, "The Code of the Streets," *The Atlantic Monthly* 273, no. 5, May 1994.

Greg Boyle, "Gang Life," *Spirituality,* Spring 1994.

George Brooks, "Let's Not Gang Up on Our Kids," *U.S. Catholic,* March 1997.

Kim Curtis, "Death Row Advice: Say No to Gangs," *San Diego Union-Tribune,* February 21, 1999.

Craig Donegan, "Preventing Juvenile Crime," *CQ Researcher,* March 15, 1996.

Laron Douglas, "In the Mind of a True Disciple," *Prison Life,* March 1995.

Blaine Harden, "With Brass-Knuckled Tales, '50's Gang Looks Back," *New York Times,* February 15, 1999.

Randi Henderson, "Caught in the Crossfire," *Common Boundary,* January/February 1995.

Ed Koch, "Get Control of Juvenile Terrorists," *American Enterprise,* May/June 1995.

Albert McGee, "Ridin' High Under the Five-Pointed Star," *Prison Life,* March 1995.

Internet Sources

ABC News, "Crime and Punishment," *Nightline,* March 27, 1998. http://archive.abcnews.go.com/sections/US/DailyNews/n10327_prisons.html.

American Medical Association, "Facts About Public Violence," June 1995. www.tyc.state.tx.us/prevention/facts-1htm.

Anti-Defamation League, "Skinheads Continue to Pose Threat to Communities in This Country," December 1, 1997. www.adl.org/pressrele/NeoSk_82/3073-82.html.

Susan Byrnes, "New Program a Lifesaver, Youth Says," *Seattle Times,* August 30, 1996. www.seattletimes.com/extra/browse/htm/luke_083096.html.

Stanley Crouch, "Bloods Are Our Local Terrorists," *New York Daily News,* October 8, 1997. www.nydailynews.com/archive/ 97.

Ann Curran, "Detroit Club Helps Kids Kick Habit," CNN Interactive, August 14, 1996. http://cnn.com/US/9608/14/kid. crime.avoidance/index.html.

Democratic Leadership Committees, "Statement of Senator Joseph R. Biden: Introduction of Crime, Youth Violence, and Drug Abuse Legislation," January 15, 1997. www.senate.gov/ ~dpc/events/970115/biden.html.

Adrienne Drell, "Parents Sue Gunmakers, Allege Sales Targeted to Gangs," *Chicago Sun-Times,* June 10, 1998. www.depaul.edu/ethics/61098a.html.

Federal Bureau of Investigation, "Gang Alert." www.fbi.gov/ kids/crimepre/gang/gang.htm.

Ted Gest with Victoria Pope, "Crime Time Bomb," *U.S. News & World Report,* March 25, 1996. www.usnews.com/usnews/ issue/crime/htm.

David G. Grant, "U.S. Grant to Help Detroit Cops Crack Down on Gangs, Violence," *Detroit News,* April 4, 1996. http://detnews. com/menu/stories/42615.htm.

Robert Greene, "Gangs, Violence in Schools," ABCNews.com Health and Living, April 12, 1998. www.abcnews.go.com/ sections/living/DailyNews/schools_violence 980412.html.

Judy Grigg Hansen, "Gang Prevention," *Boise Family Magazine,* May 1997. http://family.go.com/Features/ family_ 1997_05/bois/bois57gang.html.

Claire Johnson, Barbara Webster, and Edward Connors, "Prosecuting Gangs: A National Assessment," National Institute of Justice Research in Brief, February 1995. www.ncjrs.org/txtfiles/pgang.txt.

David Josar, "Suspect in Drug Trial Faces Death," *Detroit News,* September 15, 1995. http://detnews.com/menu/stories/ 16428.htm.

Patrick Leahy, "Democratic Youth Violence, Crime, and Drug Abuse Bill," January 15, 1997. www.senate.gov/~leahy/ e. html.

Rebecca Leung, "Taking Back the Community," ABCNews.
com, December 2, 1998. www.abcnews.go.com/sections/us/
DailyNews/gangloitering981202.html.

Duncan Levin, "Drug Dealing Rages in City Neighborhoods,"
Yale Daily News, April 20, 1995. www.cis.yale.edu/ydn/paper/
4.20.95storyno.BE.html.

Eric Lotke, "Youth Homicide: Keeping Perspective on How
Many Children Kill," *Valparaiso Law Review,* Spring 1997.
www.ncianet.org/casey.html.

Lubbock Avalanche-Journal, "Man Receives Twenty-Year
Term in Shooting Death," May 23, 1997. www.lubbockonline.
com/news/052397/man.htm.

Steve Macko, "Nationwide Survey Shows Gang Problems
Getting Worse," EmergencyNet News Service, June 22, 1996.
www.emergency.com/doj-gang.htm.

———, "Street Gang Franchises, Exporting Drugs," EmergencyNet News Service, January 21, 1996. www.emergency.
com/gangfran.htm.

John Marzulli, "Cops Bust Bloods," *New York Daily News,*
August 28, 1997. www.nydailynews.com/archive/97_08/
082797/news/3169.htm.

Anne McDermott, "Fighting Fear in the Face of Gang
Violence," CNN Interactive, August 22, 1996. http://cnn.com/
us9608/22/charlotte.loss/index.html.

———, "Snapshot of a Doomed Life: A Boy's Self-
Fulfilling Prophecy," CNN Interactive, June 27, 1996.
http://cnn.com/US/9606/27/gang.death/index.html.

Alan McEvoy, Edsel Erickson, and Norman Randolph,
"Why the Brutality?" Urban Education Web. http://eric-web.
tc.columbia.edu/administration/safety/gang_brutality.

Melanie McFarland, "Kids Under the Gun: KCTS-TV's
'Cease Fire' Looks at the Deadly Interplay of Teens and
Firearms," *Seattle Times,* October 28, 1997. www.seattletimes.
com/extra/browser/html/97/fire_102897.html.

Stephanie McLaughlin, "Ex-Coroner Aims to Build Awareness of Gangs," *Boston Globe,* March 12, 1995. www.gangwar.com/news05.htm.

Michele McPhee and Jorge Fitz-Gibbon, "Some Streets Still Killing Fields," *New York Daily News,* December 31, 1998. www.nydailynews.com/1998-1231/News_and_Views/crime/file/a-15194.asp.

National Center for Policy Analysis, "The Economics of Street Gangs." www.ncpa.org/pi/crime/july98b.html.

National Crime Prevention Council, "Securing the Future for Safer Youth and Communities." www.ncpc.org/2secfut.htm.

Office of Governor George E. Pataki, "Governor Pataki Targets Gun Traffickers Who Use Children" (press release), August 20, 1998. www.state.ny.us/governor/press/aug20_1_ 98.htm.

Office of Governor Jim Edgar, "Governor Signs Legislation Proposed by His Commission on Gangs; Protects Witnesses, Cracks Down on Leaders" (press release), June 27, 1996. www.state.il.us/gov/press/96/GANGPR.HTM.

Office of Prevention, Texas Youth Commission, "A Summary of Annual Report on School Safety Model Programs That Address Gangs." www.tyc.state.tx.us/PreventionModel_4htm.

PBS Online, *In Search of Law and Order: Reclaiming America's Kids.* 3 parts. www.pbs.org/lawandorder.

Kevin Sack, "Report Shows Growth in Hate Groups Despite Economic Boom," *New York Times,* March 3, 1998. www.codoh.com/newsdesk/9803032.html.

Paul Schwartzman, "NYPD Takes Back Streets," *New York Daily News,* May 20, 1998.

E. K. Shipp, "Nabes Can Slash Gang Activity," *New York Daily News,* October 28, 1997. www.nydailynews.com/archive.

Clark Staten, "Los Angeles Gang Attempts to Take Over Chicago Streets," *Los Angeles Times,* November 21, 1991. www.emergency.com/chgogng1.htm.

Anna M. Tinsley, "State Lawmakers Taking Steps to Crack Down on Gang Violence," *Texas News,* January 2, 1997. www.texnews.com/news/gangs010297.html.

U.S. Department of Justice, "Anti-Gang and Youth Violence Legislation: Summary of Major Provisions." www.usdoj.pov/ag/agyulg.htm.

———, "The President's Anti-Gang and Youth Violence Strategy." www.usdoj.gov/ag/anti-gang.htm.

Sharon Walsh, "Anti-Gun Forces Go After Manufacturers," *Washington Post,* April 12, 1999. www.washpost.com/wp-srv/national/longterm/gunfight/stories/guns041299.htm.

Gary Walz, "Gangs in Schools," *ERIC Clearinghouse on Urban Education Digest,* 1999. http://eric-web.tc.columbia.edu/digests/dig99.html.

Gordon Witkin, "Swift and Certain Punishment," *U.S. News & World Report,* December 29, 1997. www.usnews.com/usnews/issue/971229/29crim.htm.

Index

Picture Credits

About the Author

Lisa Wolff is a writer and editor with many years of staff experience at New York publishing houses. She currently lives in San Diego, where she edits reference books and writes articles on health and books on social issues.